How to Write
STORIES WITH
A TWIST

CREATING TWIST PLOTS for SHORT STORIES AND NOVELS

How to Write
STORIES WITH
A TWIST

· ·

CREATING TWIST PLOTS for SHORT STORIES AND NOVELS

Jane Bettany

DORMOUSE

Published by Dormouse Press, an imprint of Guidemark Publishing Limited

ISBN 978-0-9576704-8-8

A catalogue record for this book is available from the British Library.

Cover image licensed by Ingram Image

www.dormousepress.co.uk

CONTENTS

WHY TWIST?

Writing tales with a twist is a little different to writing other kinds of stories. It takes a certain skill to be able to pull off a surprise ending or sting in the tail, or develop a novel chock full of twists and turns that keep your audience hooked until the very last page.

Like all works of fiction, twist stories need certain essential ingredients, including characterisation, setting, description and dialogue. In a twist story it's the *plot* that is different, and that's going to be the main focus of this book. You're going to learn about the six different types of plot twist and discover how to use them to create your own twist fiction. Along the way, we'll analyse several story examples and explore how the mechanics of twist plots work in published fiction. We'll also consider:

- how to build a piece of fiction around a story premise or twist idea
- the importance of sowing clues
- how to misdirect your readers
- some of the twist plots to avoid, and
- how to submit your work to an editor, publisher or agent.

If you are interested in writing stories with a twist, it's highly likely that you also enjoy reading twist fiction. Stories with a twist in the tail have been popular for a very long time. Over the centuries, deceptive twists have found their way into tales such as Shakespeare's *Romeo and Juliet*, Dickens' *Great Expectations*, and formed the basis of popular short stories by authors such as O Henry and Roald Dahl. Plot twists regularly crop up in contemporary films too: who can forget the twists in movies such as *Se7en*, *The Sixth Sense*, *The Others*, and *Secret Window*?

Stories with a twist include plot developments and stings in the tail that completely change the outcome of the story. Movie-goers and readers absolutely adore these twists—whether it's in a full length novel-and-movie such as *Gone Girl* or in the flash fiction and short stories that appear regularly in magazines and online.

Literary critics, on the other hand, are often less enthusiastic about plot twists, seeing them as contrived or lacking literary merit. However, what the critics *can't* deny is that twist stories bring a huge amount of pleasure to a lot of people and, for that reason, they are enormously popular. Readers can't get enough of them.

Some people enjoy being surprised by a twist. Others like to anticipate what's going to happen and try to guess the ending (just as readers of crime fiction enjoy solving a whodunnit).

Warning - spoiler alerts!

Throughout this book I will reference the twists from a number of well-known books and films—so there are going to be a few spoilers for those of you who haven't read those novels or seen the movies.

Do the twist

Before we start to learn *how* twist stories work, let's spend a few minutes considering *why* twist stories are worth writing.

First of all, there are plenty of places to sell your work: readers love twist stories—which means that magazine editors and publishers are always on the look out to buy them. In other words, there is a *market* for them. With a few exceptions, the UK magazines that publish short stories welcome tales with a twist. In fact, many have regular slots for exactly those kind of stories. The same is true of magazine markets in North America and Australia. This is great news for writers because it means there is *demand* for this kind of story.

Novels that feature a major twist will also be of interest to many of the mainstream publishers. Now don't get me wrong—you can't rely solely on a clever plot twist to hold together a weak, poorly structured novel. You will still have to deliver a manuscript that is well-written and populated by credible, complex characters. However, what a plot twist *can* do for your novel is give it an 'edge' or help it stand out (so long as the twist isn't contrived or thrown in merely to impress). Any twist should be an integral part of the whole story.

And the second reason is... it's fun! Thinking up ideas for story twists can be thoroughly enjoyable. Sometimes an idea will strike you when you least expect it—although you'll probably need to think that idea through carefully to develop it into a workable twist plot.

When you do find a way to turn a story on its head and surprise your readers, it's akin to a eureka! moment—and very satisfying.

And finally... twist stories can help with writer's block. Writing is a wonderful pastime that is very rewarding in lots of ways. It can also be difficult and, at times, disheartening. Most writers go through frustrating periods when the words won't flow as quickly as they'd like them to. When that happens, it can knock your confidence as a writer. Your well of ideas may shrivel or dry up completely. If that happens, you'll find yourself facing a complete block.

It's during these difficult periods that many novelists turn to short story writing, and to twist stories in particular. Sometimes it can be hugely beneficial to take a break from writing a crime novel or science fiction story (or whatever it is you're working on) and concentrate instead on something completely different. Sometimes a little twist is all that's needed to overcome that block.

Let's recap

To recap, twist stories are beneficial because:

- there are plenty of places to sell your work (so it can be lucrative)
- they are fun to write (devising a twist plot can be very satisfying)
- they can help you overcome writer's block (try a twist story when your other writing projects aren't going well).

So, are you ready to get started? Let's twist!

DO YOUR RESEARCH

DO YOUR RESEARCH

If you've read my book *How to Write Short Stories That Sell*, you probably already know how passionate I am about the importance of researching writing markets *before* starting work on a piece of fiction. In my opinion, successful writers are the ones who understand the market they are writing for, and are familiar with the kind of stories that are popular with editors. That's not to say you can't try something different—on the contrary, if you can produce a story or novel that is unusual or distinctive, so much the better. However, by familiarising yourself with the latest publishing trends, you will be in a better position to gauge whether there really *is* a market for the kind of story you want to write.

One of the best ways to research markets for twist fiction is to buy or borrow copies of the magazines that publish short twist stories or—if you intend to write a novel—make sure you read the bestselling books that *everyone* is talking about (especially those with cunning twists or surprise endings).

However, even the most ingenious plot twist won't save a poorly written story. You'll still need to work hard at creating interesting characters that readers will care about. You will also need to get to grips with point of view, flashback, setting, description, and dialogue—although we won't be covering these story elements in detail in this book. Our main focus is going to be on learning how to create twist plots that you can use in short fiction and novels.

If you want to know more about the craft of writing you can learn a lot simply by reading the work of other authors. As Stephen King has said: *"If you want to be a writer, you must do two things above all others: read a lot and write a lot."* When you take that first step along the path to becoming a published writer, reading will never be quite the same again. From that moment on, you'll find yourself *analysing* the things you read. You'll be critical when something doesn't work well, and you'll be in awe of the work of truly gifted writers. And remember that you can learn as much from stories that don't work as you can from the really good ones.

Whenever you read a piece of fiction, ask yourself the following:

- Did you enjoy it? If you did, what was it that you enjoyed so much? How can you apply some of those same writing techniques to your own stories?

- Did you like the characters? Why did you like them, or why did you dislike them?

If you didn't enjoy a story, ask yourself *why* to throw up learning points for your own writing. It's not enough to say a story was boring or trashy. Dig beneath the surface of your disdain to uncover what (in your opinion) went wrong.

- Was the overall plot good, but the pace too slow or too fast?

- Maybe the pacing was right, but the characters were flawed or one-dimensional.

- Perhaps you didn't like the protagonist and, as a consequence, didn't care what happened to him.

- Did you love the first three quarters of the book but hate the ending?

- If this was your story, what exactly would you have done differently?

As you read short twist stories or novels, decide what it is *you* would like to write. If you've identified a magazine that you want to aim for, download the author guidelines from the magazine's website. These will tell you about story length and explain how to submit your work. The guidelines may even include a list of plots to avoid (something we'll consider in a later chapter). Reading the author guidelines and the stories that have appeared in recent issues of the magazine will help you to develop an appropriate writing style and improve your chances of being published.

Magazine editors clearly state the word counts they are looking for—so make sure your short story fits into that range. Novel writing, on the other hand, is far less prescriptive. Most novels are somewhere between 75,000 and 120,000 words, with 90,000 being an average. However, with novels there are always exceptions. You could write something that is 60,000 words or 150,000 words and still stand a chance of selling it, providing the publisher thinks it's well-written, fits into their list and will sell enough copies.

Find out all you can about how the publishing industry works. Both agents and publishing houses tend to specialise in a certain genre or style of novel. If you plan to weave some plot twists into a science fiction or fantasy novel, find out which agents or editors will be interested in *that* genre. If you're aiming to write a romantic story with a twist, check which of the agents might represent you or research the publishing imprints that publish similar types of novel.

Twists can be applied across any genre. Rather than looking for an agent or publisher of 'twist plots', find someone who specialises in the type of book into which your twist plot has been woven. There is, of course, no guarantee that they will be interested in your manuscript, but you will at least be sending it to someone who considers submissions in your chosen genre.

Let's recap

The best way to research the markets and understand what makes a good twist story is to read published fiction in magazines, books and online.

Now, as you start to think about ideas for your own stories, let's think about which way you're going to twist.

TYPES OF TWIST

THE UNRELIABLE NARRATOR

The first step in learning how to write a good twist story is to understand how the different twist types work. As I've already explained, twist plots crop up in many story genres: horror, science fiction, ghost stories, crime fiction and even romance—but it's not the genre we'll be thinking about in this chapter, rather the different methods of twisting a story to surprise, amaze and delight your readers.

The unreliable narrator

One of the most popular types of twist is the unreliable narrator. Whether written in the first person or the third person, most stories are told from the perspective of one protagonist or main character. As readers, we instinctively trust what that character tells us. As the story unfolds, we see the world through their eyes and we tend to take their word for things. We have belief in the main character and assume that they are telling the truth.

An *unreliable* narrator tells a story that hides the truth—sometimes intentionally, sometimes not. For instance, in the novel *Gone Girl*, the first part of the book includes excerpts from a diary written by Amy Elliott, who is one of the main characters. She writes as a loving, and yet frightened wife, revealing a series of incidents which—coupled with her disappearance—lead us to believe that she has been murdered by her husband. In this novel, the first big twist comes half way through the book when we learn that Amy isn't dead at all. The 'facts' that the reader has learned and believed in during the first part of the book are nothing more than an elaborate hoax, purposely designed to mislead. The things Amy has written in her diary are a carefully constructed web of lies. She is an unreliable narrator.

Gone Girl is a very accomplished book with a major twist and, if you haven't done so already, I'd urge you to read it (even if I have spoiled the twist for you).

Foreshadowing

The skill of building a twist around an unreliable narrator is to foreshadow things subtly without making it too easy to guess that the narrator is untrustworthy. Foreshadowing is the literary device of dropping hints about what is going to happen. In a novel with a linear plot, foreshadowing is more about intriguing readers and encouraging them to read on. In a twist story, foreshadowing is also a way to sow clues that give the reader a fair chance of guessing the twist (without making it too obvious).

When the reader is presented with the surprise ending, they should be able to look back at the foreshadowed hints and think "Oh, yes! Of course. I should have guessed." When that happens, your audience will be satisfied. On the other hand, if you don't play fair with your readers, they will be left scratching their heads and feeling disappointed and cheated. We'll discuss how to sow clues in more detail in a later chapter.

REVERSAL OF IDENTITY

Closely linked to an unreliable narrator is the twist that uses a reversal of identity. In these kind of stories one of the characters turns out to be someone (or something) else. This is another kind of twist that relies on the reader making assumptions. With a twist that relies on an unreliable narrator, the reader assumes that the narrator is telling the truth. In a reversal of identity twist, the reader makes an assumption about a character that turns out to be false.

For example, in the film *The Others*, we assume that Grace Stewart (the character played by Nicole Kidman) is alive and being haunted by ghosts. The reversal occurs in the film's finale, when it's revealed that it is Grace Stewart and her children who are the ghosts and that *they* are being plagued by the living occupants of the house.

Another example of a reversal of identity is when the hero of a story turns out to be the villain, or vice versa. Or, as in the novel *Gone Girl*, when the supposed victim turns out to be the perpetrator. The character Amy Elliott is not only an unreliable narrator, but also a classic example of a reversal of identity.

There are other examples too, such as stories that unfold only for the twist to reveal that the main character is actually an animal or inanimate object such as a car. For several reasons, this is a plot twist best avoided and I'll tell you why in a later chapter.

If you're creating a twist by using a reversal of identity, you need to make this change a credible one. Let's imagine you have a main character called Joseph who shows kindness, respect and generosity throughout the story. If you then go on to reveal that Joseph is actually a crooked, cold-hearted thief, your readers may find such a radical personality change hard to accept. To overcome this problem and to make the twist palatable, you will need to include some tell-tale character traits or weave in other clues earlier in the story. This has to be done carefully though. Don't give away too much. In these situations, the skill lies in convincing the readers that your character is honest, decent and sincere and then surprising them by *inverting* that perception as you reveal that he is actually dishonest and insincere.

To successfully deliver a reversal of character, you need to focus on the twist in your story. If the twist is that *Joseph is a thief* you will need to create the *illusion* that Joseph is honest and trustworthy. To do this, think about:

- The traits or characteristics that would lull the readers into trusting Joseph.
- Why would Joseph be considered honest?
- What would make the readers side with him?

The more convincing you can make Joseph, the more shocking it will be for readers when you unmask him as a thief.

REVERSAL OF MOTIVE

To achieve this kind of twist you will need to write a story that leads your audience to believe that a character's actions are motivated by a certain goal, only to reveal that their actions are deceitful and their goal is really something completely different (and usually more malevolent).

For example, let's imagine that you have created a character called Martha who is befriended at her tennis club by a blonde-haired woman called Fenella, who shares her interest in tennis and running. Fenella tells Martha that she's new to the area and feeling lonely without all her old friends and family around her. Martha believes that their growing friendship is genuine and trusts Fenella completely—only to discover that Fenella has been secretly stalking her husband. The apparent friendship is a ruse to steal Martha's husband and ruin her marriage. This kind of twist is commonly used in romantic suspense novels, or psychological thrillers.

In the film *Se7en*, the serial killer John Doe (played by Kevin Spacey) appears to be co-operating with the police to help them solve the last two murders. However, his real intention is to reveal that the penultimate victim is Detective Mills' pregnant wife (which prompts Mills to shoot John Doe and make him the final victim).

The reversal of motive twist frequently ends with the supposed hero turning into a villain, which can be a difficult thing to pull off successfully. As a writer you will have spent time establishing your protagonist's characteristics and, consequently, your readers will have begun to like and relate to your hero. Once that's happened, it can be hard for them to accept a complete change in personality. If you've transformed your hero into a villain or a criminal, you *must* have a good reason or clear motivation for such a radical change. As with a reversal of identity twist, to make the transition credible, you should include some foreshadowing or provide clues by giving your character certain traits that make their personality change believable, even if it's only with hindsight.

REVERSAL OF PERCEPTION

These kind of stories change the way the main character or the reader perceives things. Reversing a perception can be achieved in a few different ways.

One twist that features regularly in science fiction stories is where the main character suddenly becomes aware of 'the bigger picture'. This is often a perceptual shift in the way that he views the world he inhabits. For instance, you could have a protagonist who, through a series of investigations, discovers that the 'spaceship' he inhabits is actually an underground bunker in which the last survivors of a nuclear war are trapped. Through a series of discoveries your protagonist uncovers the truth behind an elaborate deception and sees the world as it really is.

Another classic example of a reversal of perception comes at the end of the film *Planet of the Apes*, when George Taylor (played by Charlton Heston) sees the Statue of Liberty half buried in the sand and realises that the ape-populated planet he has landed on isn't an alien planet at all, but earth 700 years in the future.

The other method is to play around with the reader's perception of a situation by introducing a non-linear narrative. This is where you tell your story either in reverse chronology, or in non-chronological order using flashbacks.

A reverse chronology is exactly what you would expect—the

plot is revealed in reverse order. It is a story told backwards. You begin by presenting the final scene or event and then go back in time to reveal and explain how that situation came about. The twist is usually delivered when the earliest chronological event is described which—because this is a reverse story—is usually in the last chapter or even the last few sentences.

Stories with a non-chronological narrative alternate between current events and things that have happened in the past. Using flashback, the story slips from the present to the past and back again to slowly reveal character motivation and the unfolding plot. To understand the truth of the story, the reader must piece together the relationship between what occurred in the flashbacks and what is happening in the story currently. You can introduce a twist by holding back vital information which is only revealed as the story reaches its climax. These kind of twists change the reader's perception of a situation or character, or explain certain actions or behaviours that, up until that point, had been a mystery. The popular TV series *Lost* used a non-linear narrative. Its mysteries and stories were revealed piece by piece over several seasons.

REVERSAL OF FORTUNE

A reversal of fortune (also known as 'peripeteia') brings a sudden change for the main character. This can be a positive change, or a negative one. An example of this kind of twist is *The Necklace* by Guy de Maupassant. This story is included in full in an upcoming chapter. If you want to avoid a spoiler, you should jump ahead and read the story now, and then return here later. If you don't want to read *The Necklace* or you are already familiar with the story, you can read on.

The Necklace is about a woman who borrows a piece of jewellery to wear to an important event. She loses the necklace and, in order to raise the money to replace it, she has to endure ten years of scrimping, hard work and poverty. Her life is ruined. Many years later she runs into the friend whose necklace she lost and finally tells her what happened. The friend then reveals that the original necklace was only costume jewellery and not real diamonds at all. The main character's decade of financial hardship has been for nothing. You can read a more detailed analysis of the story in a later chapter.

If you're going to use this kind of twist, you must make sure that the reversal of fortune stems naturally from the situation in which the character finds himself. A reversal of fortune needs to be logical, believable and connected to the rest of the story. It's

OK to use coincidence, irony, a misunderstanding, or an honest mistake to create a problem for your character from which the plot twist will arise. What you mustn't do is get your character out of a problem by using a plot device known as a *deus ex machina* (which is Latin for 'God from the machine').

Unlike a reversal of fortune, plot solutions provided by a deus ex machina are contrived, unlikely and unexpected, and unconnected to the rest of the story. Those kind of story endings leave the reader feeling cheated.

So how does a deus ex machina work?

A deus ex machina (pronounced day-oos ecks MAH-kee-nah) is when a unexpected or new character, event, object or hidden ability is suddenly called upon to solve a seemingly impossible problem. The term originated in Greek theatre and refers to scenes where a crane (the machine) was used to lower an actor playing God (deus) onto the stage to put things right at the end of the play.

Let me give you a quick example: let's imagine for a moment that your protagonist needs to fix a piece of equipment in order to make his escape, but the operating instructions for the equipment are in Cantonese. A deus ex machina would occur if your protagonist's friend (and fellow captive) suddenly declared that he understands Cantonese—even though this hasn't been mentioned before and there is no logical reason for him knowing the language.

Remember, you're a writer, not a magician pulling rabbits out of a hat. If you want your twists to work, you will need to avoid contrived or easy solutions.

In real life, people don't always get what they deserve. As a writer of fiction, you can dole out poetic justice to make sure the bad guys get their comeuppance, or you can reward virtue. You can use tragedy or even comedy to bring about an appropriate outcome or—if you want to be controversial—you could use dramatic irony and allow the good guys to fail.

REVERSAL OF ACHIEVEMENT

A great example of a reversal of achievement occurs in *The Gift of the Magi* by O Henry, which we will study in detail in the next chapter. With a reversal of achievement twist, the main character usually sets out to achieve something, only to be thwarted at the last minute by their opposite character. In *The Gift of the Magi*, the objectives of husband and wife are similar, but Jim's actions cancel out what Della has achieved through the action she has taken.

Another take on this kind of twist would be if you were to write about a Pyrrhic victory (a Pyrrhic victory is one that comes at great cost and sacrifice). So, for instance, your science fiction novel could end with a victory for the Battlelord Clan, but the only survivors of the clan are the male warriors. All of their women and children have been wiped out during the war. A victory has been achieved, but the Battlelord Clan will be extinct within thirty years.

Putting things into reverse

As you approach the end of this section, you are probably beginning to understand that the majority of twist types are referred to as 'reversals'. This is a key word to keep in mind when writing twist fiction. As an author, you must take what appears to be a straightforward story and turn it on its head to surprise the readers.

Guide them gently and unsuspectingly along a plot path that will lead to an unexpected and sometimes shocking destination.

And remember that the word 'reversal' has multiple meanings. It can mean going backwards (as in a reverse chronology), but it also refers to swapping things over or overturning them, or reordering events to reveal the truth. A 'reversal' can be a misfortune, or it can be the uncovering of another side to the story. To sum up, there are six main types of twist:

- the unreliable narrator
- reversal of identity
- reversal of motive
- reversal of perception
- reversal of fortune (AKA peripeteia)
- reversal of achievement

The best twist stories are more about reversal than they are about surprise. These types of twist allow you to reverse or change many things. You can mislead the reader into thinking that a character is a man, when actually it's a woman. The haunted can become the haunter, the victim the perpetrator, and you can transform a hero into a villain. Or you can use irony to turn the tables on a character, or cancel out their achievement, or create a situation where their sacrifice becomes worthless.

You can write a story that leads your readers to make certain assumptions about your characters and the actions that are unfolding. You can use foreshadowing techniques, or provide subtle clues, but you will have to hold back certain information so as not to reveal the whole picture. What you *shouldn't* do is try to trick the readers, or lie to them or do anything that will leave them feeling duped.

Some stories are difficult to label as belonging to any one kind of twist. They may encompass more than one type of reversal or combine a reversal with an unreliable narrator. Don't worry too much about being able to label stories by 'type'. This book isn't about testing your theoretical knowledge. It's about making you familiar with some of the different twist types so that you can use that information to develop your own story plots.

As we work through the coming chapters I'll be referring to story examples that will help you to develop a better understanding of the different types of twist.

A powerful device

Story twists are a very powerful device that can be immensely valuable for writers. When you reveal your twist, the reader has to re-examine everything they have understood about the story up to that point. I like to think of twist stories as the literary equivalent of pictorial illusions—such as the young woman / old lady image published in 1915 by the cartoonist W E Hill (take a look at the image on the next page).

When I first saw this picture I saw an old woman. It was only when I was prompted to re-examine the image that I realised it also depicted a beautiful, much younger lady. Revealing your story twist has a similar effect—suddenly, your readers see things differently.

Cartoonist W E Hill's drawing My Wife and My Mother-in-Law, *appeared in Puck magazine in November 1915. If you're struggling to see the young lady, try viewing the old woman's mouth as the young lady's necklace, the old woman's nose becomes the young lady's jaw, and the old woman's eye is the young lady's ear.*

EXAMPLE STORIES

THE GIFT OF THE MAGI - O HENRY

At this point, I think it's a good idea to study a story example. We referred to *The Gift of the Magi* when we discussed the 'reversal of achievement' twist type. This story is probably the best known work of the master of surprise endings, O Henry.

O Henry was the pen name of William Sydney Porter, an American writer born in 1862 whose life had a few twists and surprises of its own, including a spell in prison for embezzlement. He was a prolific writer of short stories and he died in 1910.

It isn't essential that you read all of the story examples that are included in this book, but reading the stories will help you to grasp the art of the twist plot much more quickly than simply reading my analysis of each piece of short fiction.

Here is *The Gift of the Magi* in full, followed by an analysis of the story, based on a model or framework designed to help you understand how twist stories are structured. As you read the story, keep in mind how events unfold and why the twist works so well.

The Gift of the Magi by O Henry

One dollar and eighty-seven cents. That was all. And sixty cents of it was in pennies. Pennies saved one and two at a time by bulldozing the grocer and the vegetable man and the butcher until one's cheeks burned with the silent imputation of parsimony that such close dealing implied. Three times Della counted it. One dollar and eighty-seven cents. And the next day would be Christmas.

There was clearly nothing to do but flop down on the shabby little couch and howl. So Della did it. Which instigates the moral reflection that life is made up of sobs, sniffles, and smiles, with sniffles predominating.

While the mistress of the home is gradually subsiding from the first stage to the second, take a look at the home. A furnished flat at $8 per week. It did not exactly beggar description, but it certainly had that word on the lookout for the mendicancy squad.

In the vestibule below was a letter-box into which no letter would go, and an electric button from which no mortal finger could coax a ring. Also appertaining thereunto was a card bearing the name "Mr. James Dillingham Young."

The "Dillingham" had been flung to the breeze during a former period of prosperity when its possessor was being paid $30 per week. Now, when the income was shrunk to $20, the letters of "Dillingham" looked blurred, as though they were thinking seriously of contracting to a modest and unassuming D. But whenever Mr. James Dillingham Young came home and reached his flat above he was called "Jim" and greatly hugged by Mrs. James Dillingham Young, already introduced to you as Della. Which is all very good.

Della finished her cry and attended to her cheeks with the powder rag. She stood by the window and looked out dully at a gray cat walking a gray fence in a gray backyard. Tomorrow would be Christmas Day, and she had only $1.87 with which to buy Jim a present. She had been saving every penny she could for months, with this result. Twenty dollars a week doesn't go far. Expenses had been greater than she had calculated. They always are. Only $1.87 to buy a present for Jim. Her Jim. Many a happy hour she had spent planning for something nice for him. Something fine and rare and sterling—something just a little bit near to being worthy of the honor of being owned by Jim.

There was a pier-glass between the windows of the room. Perhaps you have seen a pier-glass in an $8 flat. A very thin and very agile person may, by observing his reflection in a rapid sequence of longitudinal strips, obtain a fairly accurate conception of his looks. Della, being slender, had mastered the art.

Suddenly she whirled from the window and stood before the glass. Her eyes were shining brilliantly, but her face had lost its color within twenty seconds. Rapidly she pulled down her hair and let it fall to its full length.

Now, there were two possessions of the James Dillingham Youngs in which they both took a mighty pride. One was Jim's gold watch that had been his father's and his grandfather's. The other was Della's hair. Had the queen of Sheba lived in the flat across the airshaft, Della would have let her hair hang out the window some day to dry just to depreciate Her Majesty's jewels and gifts. Had King Solomon been the janitor, with all his treasures piled up in the basement, Jim would have pulled out his watch every time he passed, just to see him pluck at his beard from envy.

So now Della's beautiful hair fell about her rippling and shining like a cascade of brown waters. It reached below her knee and made itself almost a garment for her. And then she did it up again nervously and quickly. Once she faltered for a minute and stood still while a tear or two splashed on the worn red carpet.

On went her old brown jacket; on went her old brown hat. With a whirl of skirts and with the brilliant sparkle still in her eyes, she fluttered out the door and down the stairs to the street.

Where she stopped the sign read: "Mme. Sofronie. Hair Goods of All Kinds." One flight up Della ran, and collected herself, panting. Madame, large, too white, chilly, hardly looked the "Sofronie."

"Will you buy my hair?" asked Della.

"I buy hair," said Madame. "Take yer hat off and let's have a sight at the looks of it."

Down rippled the brown cascade.

"Twenty dollars," said Madame, lifting the mass with a practised hand.

"Give it to me quick," said Della.

Oh, and the next two hours tripped by on rosy wings. Forget the hashed metaphor. She was ransacking the stores for Jim's present.

She found it at last. It surely had been made for Jim and no-one else. There was no other like it in any of the stores, and she had turned all of them inside out. It was a platinum fob chain simple and chaste in design, properly proclaiming its value by substance alone and not by meretricious ornamentation—as all good things should do. It was even worthy of The Watch. As soon as she saw it she knew that it must be Jim's. It was like him. Quietness and value—the description applied to both. Twenty-one dollars they took from her for it, and she hurried home with the 87 cents. With that chain on his watch Jim might be properly anxious about the time in any company. Grand as the watch was, he sometimes looked at it on the sly on account of the old leather strap that he used in place of a chain.

When Della reached home her intoxication gave way a little to prudence and reason. She got out her curling irons and lighted the gas and went to work repairing the ravages made by generosity added to love. Which is always a tremendous task, dear friends—a mammoth task.

Within forty minutes her head was covered with tiny, close-lying curls that made her look wonderfully like a truant schoolboy. She looked at her reflection in the mirror long, carefully, and critically.

"If Jim doesn't kill me," she said to herself, "before he takes a second look at me, he'll say I look like a Coney Island chorus girl. But what could I do—oh! what could I do with a dollar and eighty-seven cents?"

At 7 o'clock the coffee was made and the fryingpan was on the back of the stove hot and ready to cook the chops.

Jim was never late. Della doubled the fob chain in her hand and sat on the corner of the table near the door that he always entered. Then she heard his step on the stair way down on the first flight, and she turned white for just a moment. She had a habit for saying little silent prayers about the simplest everyday things, and now she whispered: "Please God, make him think I am still pretty."

The door opened and Jim stepped in and closed it. He looked thin and very serious. Poor fellow, he was only twenty-two—and to be burdened with a family! He needed a new overcoat and he was without gloves.

Jim stopped inside the door, as immovable as a setter at the scent of quail. His eyes were fixed upon Della, and there was an expression in them that she could not read, and it terrified her. It was not anger, nor surprise, nor disapproval, nor horror, nor any of the sentiments that she had been prepared for. He simply stared at her fixedly with that peculiar expression on his face.

Della wriggled off the table and went for him.

"Jim, darling," she cried, "don't look at me that way. I had my hair cut off and sold because I couldn't have lived through Christmas without giving you a present. It'll grow out again—you won't mind, will you? I just had to do it. My hair grows awfully fast. Say 'Merry Christmas!' Jim, and let's be happy. You don't know what a nice—what a beautiful, nice gift I've got for you."

"You've cut off your hair?" asked Jim, laboriously, as if he had not arrived at that patent fact yet even after the hardest mental labor.

"Cut it off and sold it," said Della. "Don't you like me just as well, anyhow? I'm me without my hair, ain't I?"

Jim looked about the room curiously.

"You say your hair is gone?" he said, with an air almost of idiocy.

"You needn't look for it," said Della. "It's sold, I tell you—sold and gone, too. It's Christmas Eve, boy. Be good to me, for it went for you. Maybe the hairs of my head were numbered," she went on with sudden serious sweetness, "but nobody could ever count my love for you. Shall I put the chops on, Jim?"

Out of his trance Jim seemed quickly to wake. He enfolded his Della. For ten seconds let us regard with discreet scrutiny some inconsequential object in the other direction. Eight dollars a week or a million a year—what is the difference? A mathematician or a wit would give you the wrong answer. The magi brought valuable gifts, but that was not among them. This dark assertion will be illuminated later on.

Jim drew a package from his overcoat pocket and threw it upon the table.

"Don't make any mistake, Dell," he said, "about me. I don't think there's anything in the way of a haircut or a shave or a shampoo that could make me like my girl any less. But if you'll unwrap that package you may see why you had me going a while at first."

White fingers and nimble tore at the string and paper. And

then an ecstatic scream of joy; and then, alas! a quick feminine change to hysterical tears and wails, necessitating the immediate employment of all the comforting powers of the lord of the flat.

For there lay The Combs—the set of combs, side and back, that Della had worshipped long in a Broadway window. Beautiful combs, pure tortoise shell, with jewelled rims—just the shade to wear in the beautiful vanished hair. They were expensive combs, she knew, and her heart had simply craved and yearned over them without the least hope of possession. And now, they were hers, but the tresses that should have adorned the coveted adornments were gone.

But she hugged them to her bosom, and at length she was able to look up with dim eyes and a smile and say: "My hair grows so fast, Jim!"

And them Della leaped up like a little singed cat and cried, "Oh, oh!"

Jim had not yet seen his beautiful present. She held it out to him eagerly upon her open palm. The dull precious metal seemed to flash with a reflection of her bright and ardent spirit.

"Isn't it a dandy, Jim? I hunted all over town to find it. You'll have to look at the time a hundred times a day now. Give me your watch. I want to see how it looks on it."

Instead of obeying, Jim tumbled down on the couch and put his hands under the back of his head and smiled.

"Dell," said he, "let's put our Christmas presents away and keep 'em a while. They're too nice to use just at present. I sold the watch to get the money to buy your combs. And now suppose you put the chops on."

The magi, as you know, were wise men—wonderfully wise men—who brought gifts to the Babe in the manger. They invented the art of giving Christmas presents. Being wise, their gifts were no doubt wise ones, possibly bearing the privilege of exchange in case of duplication. And here I have lamely related to you the uneventful chronicle of two foolish children in a flat who most unwisely sacrificed for each other the greatest treasures of their house. But in a last word to the wise of these days let it be said that of all who give gifts these two were the wisest. Of all who give and receive gifts, such as they are wisest. Everywhere they are wisest. They are the magi.

Story analysis

The Gift of the Magi was first published in December 1905 and it's written in a style that was popular at the time. If the story was being written now, I'm sure there are certain sections that would be edited or removed completely. However, the structure of the story itself is quite timeless and it is a wonderful example (probably the quintessential example) of a twist story.

I want you to think about the structure of the story. Let's use the following headings as a framework to break it down into its constituent parts. You can use the same headings as a guide whenever you want to analyse a story. You can also use the framework to develop a generic outline or model on which to build your own short fiction.

OPENING: The opening sentences are where you set the scene and introduce a character (usually your main character). It's a good idea to begin the story at a moment of action, crisis or change. In *The Gift of the Magi* the opening sentences introduce us to Della, who is in crisis because she only has one dollar and eighty-seven cents with which to buy a gift for her husband, Jim.

SITUATION / IMPERATIVE: At this stage of the story you can expand on the scenario or situation described in the opening scene. Here you will provide extra evidence to give background information and support and explain the motivation and unfolding actions of your main character. In *The Gift of the Magi* the second section of the story explains that Della and Jim are young and poor, but nevertheless happy and that Della wants to buy a gift that is worthy of her husband.

FIRST CRISIS POINT: "Only $1.87 to buy a present for Jim." The dire financial position in which the couple find themselves makes it seemingly impossible for Della to achieve her goal.

CLUE: In twist stories, clues should be woven into the text wherever they fit best. In *The Gift of the Magi* the first clue is sown when the writer explains that: "There were two possessions of the James Dillingham Youngs in which they both took a mighty pride. One was Jim's gold watch that had been his father's and his grandfather's. The other was Della's hair." The story then moves on to discuss the disposal of the latter, but it is only later in the story that the significance of the watch is revealed.

ACTION / TURNING POINT: It is at this stage that the first crisis is addressed and the main character takes action to resolve the problem they are facing. There is usually no going back on the action taken at this point in the story, although further problems may well arise as a direct result of that action. In *The Gift of the Magi* Della takes the momentous decision to sell her hair.

CLUE: Here, another clue is slipped into the story. Having sold her hair, Della seeks out the ideal gift for Jim and finds a platinum fob chain. Whilst we may not necessarily recognise it as a clue, this part of the story emphasises the importance of the watch which raises its significance later on.

AFTERMATH: Having taken action in the turning point, the story goes on to explain what happens next. In our example story, Della worries about Jim's reaction to her short hair and goes about the business of preparing for his return.

CLUE: Not all stories will have another clue at this point. How and where they are introduced will depend on the kind of story and the type of twist used. In *The Gift of the Magi* there is a subtle clue when we read that "Jim stopped inside the door, as immovable as a setter at the scent of quail. His eyes were fixed upon Della, and there was an expression in them that she could not read." It is only at the end of the story, once we know the twist, that we understand Jim's reaction. He is in shock. He has *also* sacrificed something precious to obtain a special gift of combs for his wife's beautiful hair, only to come home and discover that her hair has been cut short.

There is another clue in this section of the story when we are told "Eight dollars a week or a million a year—what is the difference? A mathematician or a wit would give you the wrong answer. The magi brought valuable gifts, but that was not among them. This dark assertion will be illuminated later on." *This dark assertion will be illuminated later on.* This sentence—which hints at something to come—is an example of foreshadowing. It's a literary device that uses words or a phrase to hint that something is going to happen in order to encourage the reader to read on.

TWIST: Some stories have just one twist and, in the majority of cases, the twist comes at the end, often in the last sentence. Other stories have more than one twist. *The Gift of the Magi* could be said to have two twists—the first being the unwrapping of Jim's gift to Della. The combs: the beautiful, tortoise shell combs that Della has coveted for so long. And now she can't wear them because her hair has been cut off.

SECOND TWIST: If your story has a second twist (not all of them will have) it will usually follow swiftly on the heels of the first twist. In *The Gift of the Magi* the second and most shocking twist comes when Della presents her gift of a fob chain to Jim. It is then that he reveals that he has sold the watch to buy the combs.

You will recall that this type of twist is called a reversal of achievement. The objective the main character (Della) sets out to achieve is thwarted by her opposite number (Jim). Della has cut her hair to buy the fob chain, and Jim has sold his watch to buy the combs. Each of them has made a sacrifice out of love. That was their real gift to each other.

THE NECKLACE – GUY DE MAUPASSANT

As we studied *The Gift of the Magi*, we analysed the story using headings that formed a framework or outline. But does that same model apply to other twist stories? Or are they all different?

Let's test the theory by reading another well-known story— *The Necklace* by Guy de Maupassant. As with *The Gift of the Magi*, this story was written quite some time ago—in fact, the story is even older (it's said that Guy de Maupassant's work influenced O Henry's writing). *The Necklace* was first published in 1884 in a French newspaper, so it's the earliest example of a twist story that we will be studying in this book. Despite being over 130 years old this piece of realist fiction is nevertheless still very accessible and easy-to-read. It's an example of a 'reversal of fortune' twist, but equally you could argue that it is also a 'reversal of perception' story.

Start by reading *The Necklace* and then go on to read an analysis of the story based on the framework we devised in the previous chapter.

The Necklace by Guy de Maupassant

She was one of those pretty and charming girls born, as though fate had blundered over her, into a family of artisans. She had no marriage portion, no expectations, no means of getting known, understood, loved, and wedded by a man of wealth and distinction; and she let herself be married off to a little clerk in the Ministry of Education. Her tastes were simple because she had never been able to afford any other, but she was as unhappy as though she had married beneath her; for women have no caste or class, their beauty, grace, and charm serving them for birth or family, their natural delicacy, their instinctive elegance, their nimbleness of wit, are their only mark of rank, and put the slum girl on a level with the highest lady in the land. She suffered endlessly, feeling herself born for every delicacy and luxury.

She suffered from the poorness of her house, from its mean walls, worn chairs, and ugly curtains. All these things, of which other women of her class would not even have been aware, tormented and insulted her. The sight of the little Breton girl who came to do the work in her little house aroused heart-broken regrets and hopeless dreams in her mind. She imagined silent antechambers, heavy with Oriental tapestries, lit by torches in lofty bronze sockets, with two tall footmen in knee-breeches sleeping in large armchairs, overcome by the heavy warmth of the stove. She imagined vast saloons hung with antique silks, exquisite pieces of furniture supporting priceless ornaments, and small, charming, perfumed rooms, created just for little parties of intimate friends, men who were famous and sought after, whose homage roused every other woman's envious longings.

When she sat down for dinner at the round table covered with a three-days-old cloth, opposite her husband, who took the cover off the soup-tureen, exclaiming delightedly: "Aha! Scotch broth! What could be better?" she imagined delicate meals, gleaming silver, tapestries peopling the walls with folk of a past age and strange birds in faery forests; she imagined delicate food served in marvellous dishes, murmured gallantries, listened to with an inscrutable smile as one trifled with the rosy flesh of trout or wings of asparagus chicken.

She had no clothes, no jewels, nothing. And these were the only things she loved; she felt that she was made for them. She had longed so eagerly to charm, to be desired, to be wildly attractive and sought after. She had a rich friend, an old school friend whom she refused to visit, because she suffered so keenly when she returned home. She would weep whole days, with grief, regret, despair, and misery.

*****

One evening her husband came home with an exultant air, holding a large envelope in his hand.

"Here's something for you," he said.

Swiftly she tore the paper and drew out a printed card on which were these words: "The Minister of Education and Madame Ramponneau request the pleasure of the company of Monsieur and Madame Loisel at the Ministry on the evening of Monday, January the 18th."

Instead of being delighted, as her husband hoped, she flung the invitation petulantly across the table, murmuring: "What do you want me to do with this?"

"Why, darling, I thought you'd be pleased. You never go out, and this is a great occasion. I had tremendous trouble to get it. Everyone wants one; it's very select, and very few go to the clerks. You'll see all the really big people there."

She looked at him out of furious eyes, and said impatiently: "And what do you suppose I am to wear at such an affair?"

He had not thought about it; he stammered: "Why, the dress you go to the theatre in. It looks very nice, to me..."

He stopped, stupefied and utterly at a loss when he saw that his wife was beginning to cry. Two large tears ran slowly down from the corners of her eyes towards the corners of her mouth.

"What's the matter with you? What's the matter with you?" he faltered.

But with a violent effort she overcame her grief and replied in a calm voice, wiping her wet cheeks: "Nothing. Only I haven't a dress and so I can't go to this party. Give your invitation to some friend of yours whose wife will be turned out better than I shall."

He was heart-broken.

"Look here, Mathilde," he persisted. "What would be the cost of a suitable dress, which you could use on other occasions as well, something very simple?"

She thought for several seconds, reckoning up prices and also wondering for how large a sum she could ask without bringing upon herself an immediate refusal and an exclamation of horror from the careful-minded clerk.

At last she replied with some hesitation: "I don't know exactly, but I think I could do it on four hundred francs."

He grew slightly pale, for this was exactly the amount he had been saving for a gun, intending to get a little shooting next summer on the plain of Nanterre with some friends who went lark-shooting there on Sundays.

Nevertheless he said: "Very well. I'll give you four hundred francs. But try and get a really nice dress with the money."

The day of the party drew near, and Madame Loisel seemed sad, uneasy and anxious. Her dress was ready, however. One evening her husband said to her: "What's the matter with you? You've been very odd for the last three days."

"I'm utterly miserable at not having any jewels, not a single stone, to wear," she replied. "I shall look absolutely no-one. I would almost rather not go to the party."

"Wear flowers," he said. "They're very smart at this time of the year. For ten francs you could get two or three gorgeous roses."

She was not convinced.

"No... there's nothing so humiliating as looking poor in the middle of a lot of rich women."

"How stupid you are!" exclaimed her husband. "Go and see Madame Forestier and ask her to lend you some jewels. You know her quite well enough for that."

She uttered a cry of delight.

"That's true. I never thought of it."

Next day she went to see her friend and told her her trouble.

Madame Forestier went to her dressing-table, took up a large box, brought it to Madame Loisel, opened it, and said: "Choose, my dear."

First she saw some bracelets, then a pearl necklace, then a Venetian cross in gold and gems, of exquisite workmanship. She tried the effect of the jewels before the mirror, hesitating, unable to make up her mind to leave them, to give them up. She kept on asking: "Haven't you anything else?"

"Yes. Look for yourself. I don't know what you would like best."

Suddenly she discovered, in a black satin case, a superb diamond necklace; her heart began to beat covetously. Her hands trembled as she lifted it. She fastened it round her neck, upon her high dress, and remained in ecstasy at sight of herself.

Then, with hesitation, she asked in anguish: "Could you lend me this, just this alone?"

"Yes, of course."

She flung herself on her friend's breast, embraced her frenziedly, and went away with her treasure. The day of the party arrived.

Madame Loisel was a success. She was the prettiest woman present, elegant, graceful, smiling, and quite above herself with happiness. All the men stared at her, inquired her name, and asked to be introduced to her. All the Under-Secretaries of State were eager to waltz with her. The Minister noticed her.

She danced madly, ecstatically, drunk with pleasure, with no thought for anything, in the triumph of her beauty, in the pride of her success, in a cloud of happiness made up of this universal homage and admiration, of the desires she had aroused, of the completeness of a victory so dear to her feminine heart.

She left about four o'clock in the morning. Since midnight her husband had been dozing in a deserted little room, in company with three other men whose wives were having a good time. He threw over her shoulders the garments he had brought for them to go home in, modest everyday clothes, whose poverty clashed with the beauty of the ball-dress. She was conscious of this and was anxious to hurry away, so that she should not be noticed by the other women putting on their costly furs.

Loisel restrained her.

"Wait a little. You'll catch cold in the open. I'm going to fetch a cab."

But she did not listen to him and rapidly descended the staircase. When they were out in the street they could not find a cab; they began to look for one, shouting at the drivers whom they saw passing in the distance.

They walked down towards the Seine, desperate and shivering. At last they found on the quay one of those old nightprowling carriages which are only to be seen in Paris after dark, as though they were ashamed of their shabbiness in the daylight.

It brought them to their door in the Rue des Martyrs, and sadly they walked up to their own apartment. It was the end, for her. As for him, he was thinking that he must be at the office at ten.

She took off the garments in which she had wrapped her shoulders, so as to see herself in all her glory before the mirror. But suddenly she uttered a cry. The necklace was no longer round her neck!

"What's the matter with you?" asked her husband, already half undressed.

She turned towards him in the utmost distress.

"I... I... I've no longer got Madame Forestier's necklace..."

He started with astonishment.

"What! . . . Impossible!"

They searched in the folds of her dress, in the folds of the coat, in the pockets, everywhere. They could not find it.

"Are you sure that you still had it on when you came away from the ball?" he asked.

"Yes, I touched it in the hall at the Ministry."

"But if you had lost it in the street, we should have heard it fall."

"Yes. Probably we should. Did you take the number of the cab?"

"No. You didn't notice it, did you?"

"No."

They stared at one another, dumbfounded. At last Loisel put on his clothes again.

"I'll go over all the ground we walked," he said, "and see if I can't find it."

And he went out. She remained in her evening clothes, lacking strength to get into bed, huddled on a chair, without volition or power of thought.

Her husband returned about seven. He had found nothing.

He went to the police station, to the newspapers, to offer

a reward, to the cab companies, everywhere that a ray of hope impelled him.

She waited all day long, in the same state of bewilderment at this fearful catastrophe.

Loisel came home at night, his face lined and pale; he had discovered nothing.

"You must write to your friend," he said, "and tell her that you've broken the clasp of her necklace and are getting it mended. That will give us time to look about us."

She wrote at his dictation.

*****

By the end of a week they had lost all hope.

Loisel, who had aged five years, declared: "We must see about replacing the diamonds."

Next day they took the box which had held the necklace and went to the jewellers whose name was inside. He consulted his books.

"It was not I who sold this necklace, Madame; I must have merely supplied the clasp."

Then they went from jeweller to jeweller, searching for another necklace like the first, consulting their memories, both ill with remorse and anguish of mind.

In a shop at the Palais-Royal they found a string of diamonds which seemed to them exactly like the one they were looking for. It was worth forty thousand francs. They were allowed to have it for thirty-six thousand.

They begged the jeweller not to sell it for three days. And they arranged matters on the understanding that it would be taken back for thirty-four thousand francs, if the first one were found before the end of February.

Loisel possessed eighteen thousand francs left to him by his father. He intended to borrow the rest.

He did borrow it, getting a thousand from one man, five hundred from another, five louis here, three louis there. He gave notes of hand, entered into ruinous agreements, did business with usurers and the whole tribe of money-lenders. He mortgaged the whole remaining years of his existence, risked his signature without even knowing if he could honour it, and, appalled at the agonising face of the future, at the black misery about to fall upon him, at the prospect of every possible physical privation and moral torture, he went to get the new necklace and put down upon the jeweller's counter thirty-six thousand francs.

When Madame Loisel took back the necklace to Madame Forestier, the latter said to her in a chilly voice: "You ought to have brought it back sooner; I might have needed it."

She did not, as her friend had feared, open the case. If she had noticed the substitution, what would she have thought? What would she have said? Would she not have taken her for a thief?

*****

Madame Loisel came to know the ghastly life of abject poverty. From the very first she played her part heroically. This fearful debt must be paid off. She would pay it. The servant was dismissed. They changed their flat; they took a garret under the roof.

She came to know the heavy work of the house, the hateful duties of the kitchen. She washed the plates, wearing out her pink nails on the coarse pottery and the bottoms of pans. She washed the dirty linen, the shirts and dish-cloths, and hung them out to dry on a string; every morning she took the dustbin down into the street and carried up the water, stopping on each landing to get her breath. And, clad like a poor woman, she went to the fruiterer, to the grocer, to the butcher, a basket on her arm, haggling, insulted, fighting for every wretched halfpenny of her money.

Every month notes had to be paid off, others renewed, time gained. Her husband worked in the evenings at putting straight a merchant's accounts, and often at night he did copying at twopence-halfpenny a page.

And this life lasted ten years.

At the end of ten years everything was paid off, everything, the usurer's charges and the accumulation of superimposed interest.

Madame Loisel looked old now. She had become like all the other strong, hard, coarse women of poor households. Her hair was badly done, her skirts were awry, her hands were red. She spoke in a shrill voice, and the water slopped all over the floor when she scrubbed it. But sometimes, when her husband was at the office, she sat down by the window and thought of that evening long ago, of the ball at which she had been so beautiful and so much admired.

What would have happened if she had never lost those jewels? Who knows? Who knows? How strange life is, how fickle! How little is needed to ruin or to save!

One Sunday, as she had gone for a walk along the Champs-Elysees to freshen herself after the labours of the week, she caught sight suddenly of a woman who was taking a child out for a walk. It was Madame Forestier, still young, still beautiful, still attractive.

Madame Loisel was conscious of some emotion. Should she speak to her? Yes, certainly. And now that she had paid, she would tell her all. Why not?

She went up to her.

"Good morning, Jeanne."

The other did not recognise her, and was surprised at being thus familiarly addressed by a poor woman.

"But... Madame..." she stammered. "I don't know... you must be making a mistake."

"No... I am Mathilde Loisel."

Her friend uttered a cry.

"Oh!... my poor Mathilde, how you have changed!..."

"Yes, I've had some hard times since I saw you last; and many sorrows... and all on your account."

"On my account!... How was that?"

"You remember the diamond necklace you lent me for the ball at the Ministry?"

"Yes. Well?"

"Well, I lost it."

"How could you? Why, you brought it back."

"I brought you another one just like it. And for the last ten years we have been paying for it. You realise it wasn't easy for us; we had no money... Well, it's paid for at last, and I'm glad indeed."

Madame Forestier had halted.

"You say you bought a diamond necklace to replace mine?"

"Yes. You hadn't noticed it? They were very much alike."

And she smiled in proud and innocent happiness.

Madame Forestier, deeply moved, took her two hands.

"Oh, my poor Mathilde! But mine was imitation. It was worth at the very most five hundred francs!..."

Story analysis

OPENING: The opening section of this story is relatively long, compared to contemporary short fiction. The scene introduces the main character, Mathilde Loisel, who is dissatisfied, unhappy and longs to swap her ordinary existence for a life of luxury. Mathilde feels unfulfilled and sees herself existing in a life of drudgery.

SITUATION / IMPERATIVE: Into this scenario enters Monsieur Loisel, carrying an invitation to an important event. Mathilde's reaction shows that she is spoilt and resentful of her situation and her husband's lack of income. She wants to go to the party, but she has nothing to wear. Reluctantly, Monsieur Loisel agrees that Mathilde can spend some of their precious savings on a new dress.

FIRST CRISIS POINT: Despite acquiring a new dress, Mathilde is still not satisfied. She wants some fine jewels to wear with the dress. Monsieur Loisel suggests that Mathilde borrow something from her rich friend, Madame Forestier.

CLUE: The piece of jewellery Mathilde chooses is described as a "superb diamond necklace" and, whilst the reader has no reason at this stage to question this, the situation does perhaps give rise to a sense of unease in the reader's mind. There is an almost inevitable expectation that the necklace will be lost.

ACTION / TURNING POINT: Mathilde has a wonderful time at the party, but when she and her husband return to their home in the Rue des Martyrs (and that street name surely provides a clue of what is about to happen) Mathilde discovers that she has lost the necklace. Despite every effort to recover the jewellery, the Loisel's have no luck and have to finance an expensive replacement.

AFTERMATH: Having borrowed 36,000 francs to buy the replacement necklace, the Loisel's are pitched into a life of abject poverty. At the beginning of the story, as Mathilde observes her Breton maid, she longs for superior possessions and a better life.

Now, her old life seems almost luxurious in comparison. Mathilde finally understands the meaning of drudgery. The Breton maid is dismissed and the Loisel's are forced to work to pay off their debts. They leave the flat that Mathilde had derided and move into a garret. Mathilde has to do the heavy housework and the "hateful kitchen duties". This situation continues for ten years and the Loisel's become changed during that time. Mathilde pays twice for her mistake—firstly with money, and secondly with her lost beauty.

TWIST: There is only one twist in this story and it comes at the very end. Mathilde runs into her friend after many years and explains that her changed appearance is due to the hard times she has suffered since they last met. She describes the loss of the jewellery and its replacement—only to be told by her friend that the original necklace was made from imitation diamonds and was worth no more than five hundred francs. This twist reveals that Mathilde's years of poverty and hardship have been for nothing. Her sacrifice becomes worthless.

SECOND TWIST: Technically, there is no second twist in *The Necklace*. However, the story is loaded with themes (such as the deceptiveness of appearances) and symbolism (the necklace may be worthless, but it is still beautiful). As they finish the story, readers will reflect on the fact that Mathilde assumed the diamonds in the necklace were real, simply because it was owned by her rich friend. Mathilde, who ironically believed that she was worth more than the lowly family she was born into, spends ten years paying for a necklace that she believed was more valuable than it really was.

WRITING YOUR STORY

LET'S TWIST

Now that we've studied some story examples, it's time to start thinking about how *you* are going to create your own twist endings. One of the easiest ways to do this is to begin by thinking of a twist—but where do ideas for those twist plots come from?

In my experience, most twist ideas emerge from a simple, basic idea or story premise:

- What if a woman borrowed an expensive necklace and then lost it? (*The Necklace* by Guy de Maupassant).
- What if a woman did something drastic in order to buy a precious gift for her husband? (*The Gift of the Magi* by O Henry).
- What if someone who is obsessed with competitions gives up just before their big win? (my story *No Competition*, which you can read later in this chapter).
- What is the best way for someone to dispose of the weapon they've used to murder their spouse? (*Lamb to the Slaughter* by Roald Dahl).
- When a woman disappears, all the evidence suggests she has been murdered by her husband, but what if that isn't true? (*Gone Girl* by Gillian Flynn).

Now try to think of an idea or story premise of your own. One of the best ways to do this is to ask 'what if?' Alternatively, you can start with a straightforward statement and see where it leads you. Here are a few examples—and you can use any of these to develop a story if you can't think of an idea of your own:

- What if the woman you believed was your mother turns out not to be?
- What if the car you bought recently turns out to be a stolen vehicle?
- What if the person that moves in next door to you is someone you recognise from the past?
- What if someone becomes trapped in a lift in an abandoned building?
- What happens when someone buys a powerful motorbike in a bid to recapture their lost youth?

Next, take your idea (or use one of the ideas above) and think about how you can give it a twist or turn it on its head. In order to surprise your readers, try to get inside their heads to understand how they might think. What would be the likely human responses to each of the scenarios above? What assumptions would readers make about those situations?

Let's consider this one: *What if a woman borrowed an expensive necklace and then lost it?* Most people in this situation would confess to the owner that they had lost the jewellery. But what if the character in your story is too proud or foolish to do that?

There is an assumption that the description of the necklace is accurate—that it really was expensive. But what if that weren't true? What if the diamonds were imitation?

Let's think about another one: *A man becomes trapped in a lift in an abandoned building.* Most people in that situation would use their mobile phone to call for help. But what if there was no signal within the lift shaft? What if the man's phone had been stolen? What if the story was set in the 1960s?

Most readers would assume that, sooner or later, someone would go looking for the man and rescue him. But what if no-one knows where he is? What if he's been left there on purpose by someone who means him harm? What if he's trapped in the lift with a bee and he will get an anaphylactic reaction if he's stung? (By the way, that last scenario would probably be pushing things a bit too far—but my point is that you may need to think of and dismiss numerous scenarios before finding exactly the right twist). Whilst one idea may not work, it could give rise to another scenario that would make a brilliant twist.

Eliminate the obvious

The first plot twists or twist endings you come up with are likely to be the obvious ones. Once you've thought of them, put them aside. Push yourself to think instead of another more imaginative way to twist the story and, if necessary, discard that idea too. Keep thinking and twisting and turning and, finally, something amazing will slot into place.

Your aim should be to achieve a twist that is believable but not likely to be guessed, not even by aficionados of twist ending stories.

Let's twist again

Well-written stories with a good twist are very marketable. Well-written stories with a *double* twist are even more likely to sell.

Having surprised your reader once, why not take another look at your story to see if you can introduce a second twist?

In this chapter I'm going to share a very short story with you that will always have a place in my heart. This piece of flash fiction is by no means complex or sophisticated, but I'm fond of it because it's the first story I ever had published (back in 1992). It's a good example of a double twist, which is why I've decided to include it in this book.

No Competition by Jane Bettany

"This is getting out of hand," Edward said, inspecting the package which stood in the centre of the kitchen. "We've already got a perfectly good washing machine. What on earth possessed you to buy another one?"

Margaret twisted her hands together and bit her lip. "It was the competition," she replied. "There was a chance to win a car."

"You mean you've spent hundreds of pounds on something we don't need just to enter a competition?"

Margaret nodded.

Edward sighed and shook his head. "It's become an obsession with you, hasn't it?"

"I... don't know what you mean..." Margaret protested feebly.

"This is what I mean." He threw open a cupboard door, exposing an array of brightly coloured cans. "For instance," he said, reading from one of the labels, "*Win a weekend for two in New York. This is dog food, Margaret. For pity's sake! We've haven't got a dog."

"I take the labels off and give the cans to the animal rescue centre."

"That's not the point. You're spending a fortune on things we don't need—just to enter competitions you'll never win."

"I'm bound to win something eventually."

"No, Margaret. No. It's got to stop. I'm worried about you. Perhaps you should see a doctor... maybe even a psychiatrist."

Margaret began to cry. "I only do it because I'm bored," she said. "I keep hoping I'll win lots of money so that you can retire. I wouldn't feel so lonely then."

Edward took her hand and slipped an arm around her waist. "I'd love to retire and spend my days with you," he said, "but it just isn't possible right now."

He tilted her chin upwards and smiled down into her tear-stained face. "I'll make a deal with you," he offered. "If you promise to stop entering competitions, I'll take you on holiday somewhere... New York if you'd really like to go there."

Margaret pulled a crumpled handkerchief from her sleeve and blew her nose noisily. "Do you mean it?"

"Of course I do." Edward grinned. "It'll probably be cheaper in the long run. Providing that you send this back, of course." He tapped the unwrapped washing machine pointedly.

"OK." Margaret nodded and returned his smile. "You're right. I suppose it's all for the best."

"You arrange for the washing machine to be collected," said Edward, "and I'll organise our holiday."

****

In the electrical shop, the assistant looked very sceptical.

"There's been a mistake you see," Margaret explained. "My husband had ordered a new washing machine as well... and of course we don't need two."

She could see that they didn't believe her. The whole situation was most embarrassing. Margaret didn't like telling lies, but this was one occasion when the truth just wouldn't do.

Begrudgingly, the shop assistant agreed to collect the washing machine and Margaret retreated gratefully, making her way instinctively into the supermarket next door.

Inside the air-conditioned store, Margaret became an addict in need of a fix. Gazing longingly at the shelves of packets and cans, she was tempted by a tin of spaghetti with bold red letters emblazoned across its label. *£10,000 jackpot! Open this can to find out if you're the lucky winner.*

As she reached for the shelf she saw that her hand was trembling.

What was she doing? She didn't like spaghetti and Edward only ate the proper sort, never the tinned variety.

She lifted the can.

What about her promise? Edward was taking her to New York. She'd made a bargain. He was right, she had to stop buying these things.

"Excuse me. I'd like to get to that shelf."

The voice snapped at Margaret's indecision.

"Sorry," she said, looking at the harassed young woman and her grizzling toddler who was squirming in the seat of a shopping trolley.

"Shush, Jamie," the woman said, as the child's whimpering increased in volume.

Margaret stood with the tin in her hand, blocking the shelf.

The young woman sighed impatiently. "If you don't mind, I'm in a hurry. If you're not going to move, perhaps you could pass me a tin of that spaghetti."

"You can have this one," Margaret said, overcoming her indecision. "I can't stand the stuff."

Margaret felt ridiculously proud as she handed the can to the dumbfounded woman and walked calmly out of the supermarket.

****

As was usual when he was hungry, Jamie was making an awful racket. The cutlery drawer rattled as Mollie fumbled for the tin opener. It would have been nice to have taken Jamie for something to eat in town, but she couldn't afford such luxuries. Instead, they had ignored their rumbling stomachs and trudged back to the flat. Now Mollie was preparing spaghetti on toast.

She was so hungry and in such a rush, that she didn't notice the words printed on the inside of the jagged tin lid. *YOU HAVE WON £10,000.* She simply slopped the spaghetti into a saucepan, placed two slices of bread into the toaster, and tossed the empty can into the bin.

Story analysis

Let's take our story model and apply it to *No Competition*.

OPENING: As with *The Gift of the Magi*, this story begins at a moment of crisis and action. Edward is confronting Margaret about why she has bought a new washing machine when they don't need one. The washing machine stands in the centre of the kitchen, which provides us with a setting for the story.

SITUATION / IMPERATIVE: The next section of the story expands on and explains the scenario described in the opening scene. Margaret has a compulsion for contests and prize draws and is buying things that she doesn't need in order to enter competitions (at the time the story was written, it was common for big prizes to be offered on tinned goods using a slogan such as *open the tin to find out if you're a winner*). Clearly something needs to happen to help Margaret overcome the problem.

FIRST CRISIS POINT: Edward tells Margaret that she will have to see a doctor unless she is willing to take action to return the washing machine to the store.

CLUE: Margaret's objective is to win some money so that Edward can retire. Clearly she sees winning money as a solution to her underlying problem of loneliness.

ACTION / TURNING POINT: Margaret arranges for the store to collect the unwanted washing machine and then she slips into a nearby supermarket, where the temptation to buy goods makes her feel like "an addict in need of a fix". Will she resist temptation or will she buy the tin of spaghetti?

CLUE: Margaret has a competitor for the tin of spaghetti in the form of Mollie, a single mother obviously far more in need of a competition win than Margaret is. Margaret doesn't simply return the tin she has been looking at to the shelf—she passes the can *she* was thinking of buying over to Mollie.

AFTERMATH: For the aftermath of this story, the action moves to a different viewpoint—that of Mollie who is now in possession of the tin of spaghetti.

CLUE: We are told that Mollie is hard up, which suggests that she could do with a financial boost. This leads the reader to think: "Wouldn't it be great if she was the one to win the £10,000?"

TWIST: The first twist is that it was the tin of spaghetti that Margaret handed over that turned out to be the winning can. Had

Margaret bought that tin, she would have achieved her ambition of winning some money. When I set out to write this story, I was going to make this the only twist. My plan was to give the hard up Mollie the money instead of Margaret. But as I began to write the last few sentences, a second twist popped into my mind—without which, the story probably wouldn't have succeeded.

SECOND TWIST: The second twist in this story is that the financially strapped Mollie has the winning can in her hands—but she is so stressed and rushed that she doesn't even notice. Instead, she throws the can into the bin and no-one wins the money—neither Margaret nor Mollie.

Let's recap

In *No Competition* the twist comes when the tin of spaghetti Margaret is holding turns out to be the winning can. In fact, this is more of an ironic ending than a twist. The second and most effective twist in the story comes when Mollie fails to notice that the tin is a winner. Instead of claiming her £10,000 prize, she throws the empty can into the trash.

If you can, always try to deliver a second twist. It will make the story more satisfying for your readers, and give it a better chance of being accepted by an editor.

And why stop at a second twist? Why not try for a third, or even a fourth? Four twists would be difficult to achieve in a short story, but a series of twists is something that works very well in a novel. It can make for a real 'roller coaster' of a story that is guaranteed to keep readers turning the pages until they reach the story's conclusion.

BUILDING YOUR STORY

Once you have an idea for a twist, the next step is to build a story that will bring your plot and characters to the point at which you can deliver your surprise ending.

Let's image that when Roald Dahl wrote *Lamb to the Slaughter*, he began with the idea of finding the perfect way for a killer to get rid of a murder weapon. In order to build a story around that outcome, he would have needed to imagine the following:

- The perfect, disposable murder weapon (Dahl decided to use a frozen leg of lamb which he disposed of by getting the police to eat the evidence).

- A murder victim and a murderer (which, in the case of *Lamb to the Slaughter* was a husband and wife).

- A plausible reason or motive for the wife to kill her husband (the wife was six months pregnant and the husband had told her he was leaving her).

- A reason why the police would eat a meal at her home (Roald Dahl made the husband a policeman—so it was logical that his colleagues would be invited by the "widow" to stay and take a meal while they were at the crime scene).

Now let's go back to the scenario we considered earlier: *A man becomes trapped in a lift in an abandoned building.* If you were using this scenario to create a twist ending story, what would you need to imagine? How about:

- The situation that caused the building to become abandoned (perhaps the man was the CEO of a failed business and the building had once served as the company HQ).

- A reason for the man (let's call him Bob) to visit the building. Maybe a colleague or business partner called and asked to meet him there.

- A reason why Bob would use the lift rather than the stairs (you could give him a bad back or arthritic knees, or maybe he wants to visit his old executive office on the top floor of a twenty storey building, which is accessed using a private elevator).

- A plausible reason for the lift/elevator to break down. Perhaps cash flow problems within the business meant that the bills for building maintenance went unpaid and the lift hadn't been serviced for months.

- An explanation of why no-one knew Bob was going to the building, and why no-one will go looking for him. The most likely scenario is that Bob didn't tell anyone because he didn't want them to know. Perhaps he called at the building on his way to the airport and he is due to fly off for a two week holiday—alone. No-one will miss Bob because no-one will realise when he misses his flight.

- Most importantly of all, you need to decide on a twist. The most obvious one is that the lift doesn't break down at all, but is tampered with by an employee or disgruntled, vengeful business partner who blames Bob for the financial failure of the business. Or what if Bob has been syphoning off money from the business for years and someone has found out? It could be that someone from within the company (let's call him Frank) has noticed some discrepancies and agrees to keep quiet in exchange for a pay-off. Bob agrees to a deal and arranges to meet his blackmailer in the empty office block, but rather than hand over a case full of cash, he decides to kill Frank before heading off to the airport to make his escape.

- The twist—and Bob's downfall—could be when the lift breaks down due to poor maintenance (ironically Frank was always pestering Bob to sign the document to renew the maintenance contract, but Bob always chose to ignore him). Bob is a type 1 diabetic and, trapped in the lift, his blood sugar levels begin to drop. Eventually a lack of insulin, water and food send him into a diabetic coma. As Bob slips into the coma his last thought is that no-one will find him because he has made such a thorough job of making sure no-one knows where he is.

This scenario would need a lot more work, but it's a framework that could easily be developed into a piece of short fiction with a twist ending that will make sure Bob gets his comeuppance.

Writing exercise

Now it's time for you to develop your own twist idea. Using the story premise you created in the last chapter, or using one of the scenarios provided, start to develop the idea to build and imagine the story that will lead to your twist.

CREATING AN OUTLINE

Once you have thought of a twist and developed a scenario to fit (or vice versa), you are ready to start writing your story. Some people prefer to launch straight in and start writing without relying on an outline. Others prefer to plan their story carefully so that they know exactly where it's going before they begin to write.

If you are a 'seat of the pants' writer who likes to dive right in, then it's at this stage that you should start writing. If you are more of a planner and need help putting together an outline, here's what I recommend.

Remember the way we broke down and analysed the stories we studied earlier? Let's take the same framework headings but, instead of using them to break down and analyse a story, we're going to use them to build and create a story outline based on the 'man in the lift' scenario.

OPENING: Bob is glad that he's arranged to meet Frank in his old office block. It will give him one last chance to see the place from which he ran his business empire before he heads out of the country for good.

SITUATION / IMPERATIVE: Bob has been syphoning money out of his business for years and now the business has gone bust.

79

Frank has discovered Bob's secret but says he'll keep quiet if Bob pays him $500,000.

FIRST CRISIS POINT: Bob can afford to pay Frank—the money doesn't bother him. What worries him is whether he can trust Frank to keep his mouth shut.

CLUE: As Bob enters the building he heads for the private lift, glad that it is still working because his arthritic knees aren't up to climbing all those stairs. Bob decides he'll have to do something to improve his fitness once he moves abroad. It is at this point that his diabetes is mentioned.

ACTION / TURNING POINT: Frank is waiting for Bob in the executive office on the top floor. Bob is carrying a case, which Frank believes holds $500,000 cash. In fact, it holds a gun, fitted with a silencer, which Bob uses to silence Frank once and for all.

CLUE: Bob feels very little remorse. It's not as if he liked Frank. The two of them never got on. Frank was a pest, always nagging at him to approve a contract or sign a document.

AFTERMATH: Bob knows that Frank lives alone and his body is likely to lie undiscovered for several days. In a few hours Bob will be in the Cayman Islands. No-one will be able to prove he had anything to do with Frank's death. He takes one last look around his office before heading back to the elevator which will take him to the private, underground parking lot.

Bob's last insulin shot was first thing that morning and he hasn't eaten any breakfast. He begins to feel a little shaky and tired, and his palms are clammy. Is he just nervous, or have his blood sugar levels dropped?

TWIST: Between floors 12 and 11 the lift stops. Bob is stuck. No-one knows he is there, and no-one can *know* he has been there. He can't call anyone, and anyway his cell phone has no signal in the elevator shaft. As the building is empty, the emergency phone line in the elevator is no longer connected. Despite his bad knees, Bob jumps up and down to try and get the elevator started again. He waits. Thinks. Wonders: what is worse? Being uncovered as a murderer, or being left to die in a broken down elevator? No-one will find Bob because he has made such a thorough job of making sure no-one knows where he is.

SECOND TWIST: As Bob slowly drifts into a diabetic coma, he remembers that one of the things Frank had pestered him to sign was a contract for the maintenance of the private lift.

A well-rounded story

It's important to create a well-balanced, finely tuned piece of fiction that will hold the reader's interest throughout the story rather than simply relying on an amazing twist ending. Unless the story works well as a whole and includes believable characters and interesting action, no-one will bother reading to the end—so it won't matter how fabulous or mind-blowing your twist is. If readers abandon your story part way through, your clever twist ending will be totally wasted.

And always respect your readers. Don't deliver a twist that makes them feel tricked or deceived or feeling that you've wasted their time. Your readers will consider the minutes or hours they spend reading your story as a worthwhile investment—but only if you provide them with value by delivering a well-rounded story.

SOWING CLUES

A good plot twist has the ability to surprise or even shock readers. The best twist stories are often those that keep you guessing right until the end. However, whilst some people are quite content with being surprised, others pride themselves on being able to guess even the cleverest of twist endings (I have to confess that I fall into this category). What both kinds of readers have in common is the need to be able to look back or re-read the story once the twist has been revealed and think: "Ah! I should have guessed. Why didn't I see that?" or "Of course! I knew it!" Reactions like that stem from reader satisfaction and appreciation for the twist you have created.

In order to achieve that kind of response, you will need to scatter clues throughout your story that can be recognised (with hindsight) as signposts that point towards an inevitable outcome.

Don't make the clues too obvious though. If your audience guesses the twist early on, you'll fail to achieve the surprise you are aiming for. In fact, the reader may well skip ahead to the end to find out if they were right and then not bother reading the rest of the story.

One way to bury important clues is to drop them into the story at a time when something else is happening and the reader's mind is focused on the unfolding action, rather than on the other piece of seemingly insignificant (but vitally important) information you have provided.

As the story's creator, you must keep the twist in mind constantly as you write. Unlike the readers, *you* know exactly what is going to happen and fully understand that things aren't as they appear to be. This knowledge will influence your descriptions and general choice of words, and may even affect your writing style and tone of voice. These factors will allow you to subtly develop your twist and gradually build towards a 'big reveal', whilst avoiding anything that rings as untrue. If you can pull this off, your readers will accept the twist when it comes.

Chekhov's gun

If you're a writer of twist fiction or mystery or crime stories, sooner or later you'll come across the expression 'Chekhov's gun', a term coined when Anton Chekhov said:

> *"Remove everything that has no relevance to the story. If you say in the first chapter that there is a rifle hanging on the wall, in the second or third chapter it absolutely must go off. If it's not going to be fired, it shouldn't be hanging there."*

Anton Chekhov

What Chekhov meant by this is that you should only place something on the stage—or in a story—if it is going to be used. The presence of a rifle suggests to the audience that it will be significant to the plot. If the gun isn't going to be fired, then it isn't needed and shouldn't be there in the first place.

This principle is worth remembering as you place clues within your own stories and do your best to misdirect the readers. If you introduce your own version of 'Chekhov's gun' by mentioning something small or seemingly insignificant, make sure you make use of it before the story ends. If you take the trouble to mention something *specifically*, even if it's only subtly or in passing, it should matter to your plot. The reader won't know how or why you have included a small detail in your story until later, when its significance will be revealed. No part of your short story or novel should be irrelevant or wasteful, and you shouldn't make promises that you don't intend to keep.

Bear the Chekhov's gun principle in mind if you are foreshadowing a future event. If you draw too much attention to the 'loaded gun on the wall' or whatever it is that you intend to use later in the story, you will make things too obvious and take away the element of surprise.

THE ART OF MISDIRECTION

You may decide to throw in a few red herrings in order to misdirect or distract the reader. As I'm sure you know, a red herring is a false clue or a piece of information that is included to lead both the story's protagonist and the reader to an incorrect conclusion.

Red herrings (not to be confused with the 'Chekhov's gun' principle) distract the reader from the main plot by making certain other things seem more significant than they really are. Red herrings are most commonly used in mystery or detective fiction but, used sparingly, they can also be useful in twist stories. For example, if one of your plot twists relies on the fact that someone has revealed a secret, you could throw the blame onto a character (let's call her Liz) who you have established as a nosy gossip. But the gossiping Liz could be a red herring. The person who actually revealed the secret could be someone else entirely, ideally the person the readers will least expect.

As well as red herrings, you can use other ways to misdirect your audience to exploit conventions, assumptions and reader expectations. This tactic is often employed in stories that lead the reader to believe that the protagonist is female, when in fact they are male (or vice versa). Or you can use the different ages of characters to play around with assumptions and introduce a twist. To show you what I mean, I have included one of my own flash fiction stories as an example in this chapter. The story is called *Subject for Debate*. Read it now. It should only take a few minutes.

Subject for Debate by Jane Bettany

"Hey, Mum, only a few weeks until uni begins. Yeay!"

My daughter and I are sitting out in the garden enjoying an unusually warm day in late September. We haven't had much time together this summer—Becky has spent most of the holidays hanging out with her friends. All in all, we haven't had a proper chance to talk, she and I.

I look at her now; young and bubbly and enthusiastic. Glowing with pride. There is a palpable sense of vitality about Becky. She's buzzing with this whole university thing. I wish I could say the same.

"It's going to be sooo cool." She sips a tumbler of lemonade, rattling ice cubes against the glass.

"Certainly is." I try hard to inject some energy into my voice, but clearly I fail because Becky looks at me and frowns.

"You could try to sound a bit more enthusiastic, Mum."

"Sorry, love. I haven't quite got used to the idea, that's all."

She raises an eyebrow and then grabs hold of my hand and gives it a shake.

"Trust me. It's going to be brilliant."

"You're right." I nod. "Of course you are. It's just... well... do you really think English Literature is the right thing to study? There's still time to change."

"Mum!" Becky sighs. "You and I spent hours talking over the course options. English Literature was always the clear winner."

I nod to show that I agree, but doubt still pecks away at me.

"Come on, Mum. You love literature as much as I do. You were always reading stories to me when I was little."

I smile at the memory.

"I know. But I do wonder how much use a degree in English Literature is going to be... what sort of career is it likely to lead to do you think?"

"There are loads of jobs out there for people with an English degree."

She sounds so positive; it's infectious.

"In my opinion," she adds, "The most important thing for any student is to choose a subject they enjoy."

I'm not sure that I agree with that philosophy. But my daughter is young and I'm almost forty. For teenagers, university is a chance to spread their wings and have a good time. I'm more practical.

"I read recently that employers prefer people with degrees in subjects like business studies or marketing."

Becky shakes her head. Firmly. "It's too late to change now, Mum."

She's right, of course. It's silly of me to question things at this stage. But I do so want everything to be perfect. I left school at sixteen. Staying on to do A Levels wasn't an option for me. It's something I've come to regret over the years. No-one from my family has ever been to university. Until now.

I watch as Becky swats away a wasp that is homing in on her lemonade. She does it fearlessly, not in the least bit worried about getting stung. I wish I had her self-confidence.

"Mum," she says, "I wish you'd stop worrying. It'll be great. You'll see."

"That's what your dad says. He reckons I'm being a fusspot, worrying over nothing, as usual."

"And he's right. I can't wait to go to uni."

I laugh and squeeze her hand. "All in good time. You've got your A Levels to do first."

"And by then you'll be in your final year." She giggles and shakes her head. "I still can't get my head round it. My mum. About to become a student."

"Mature student," I correct her. "It's taken me a long time to get started, but better late than never."

"You'll love it, Mum. I know you will."

And I smile. Because she's so sure. So confident. And of course she's absolutely right.

How the story works

Subject for Debate is an example of a reversal of identity twist. The story introduces two characters—mother and daughter—who are having a conversation about the university term that is about to begin. We assume that it is the daughter who is about to start a course at university. The mother is nervous—which is a natural emotion for any mother whose daughter is about to become a student. The twist in this story is that it is the *mother* who is about to begin the course.

This story plays on social norms—it's usual for people to go to university when they are in their late teens and it's normal and natural for mothers to worry about their children. The story takes the assumptions the reader will make (based on those norms) and uses them to create a misdirection.

There are clues which are easy to pick out once you know the twist. For instance, when Becky says: *"You could try to sound a bit more enthusiastic, Mum."* At the first reading, we assume that Becky means that her mother could sound a bit more enthusiastic about the prospect of her daughter going off to university. Once we know the twist, we realise that the real subtext of what Becky is saying is: *"Come on, Mum. You're about to achieve a long held ambition by going off to university. Try to sound a bit more enthusiastic about it."*

When the protagonist says: *"Do you really think English Literature is the right thing to study? There's still time to change."* we assume that she is questioning her daughter's choice, when in fact she is questioning her own decision. Becky responds by saying: *"Mum! You and I spent hours talking over the course options. English Literature was always the clear winner."* Again, this is a suitably ambiguous statement that could apply to either mother or daughter. A more natural reaction from Becky might have been: *"Mum! You've always wanted to study English Literature."* That would certainly have been more clear, but it would also have given the game away.

Things are muddied even further when Becky says: *"Come on, Mum. You love literature as much as I do. You were always reading stories to me when I was little."* This sentence moves the attention to Becky intentionally. Just in case anyone's suspicions have been roused, this statement seems to suggests that it is, after all, Becky who is going off to study English Literature. In case there is any doubt, the reader is misdirected again when the protagonist says: *"My daughter is young and I'm almost forty. For teenagers, university is a chance to spread their wings and have a good time. I'm more practical."* This sentence reassures the reader that this is a middle-aged mother who is fretting about the imminent departure of her child.

For those who are good at guessing twists, the following sentence could have been a giveaway: *"She's right, of course. It's silly of me to question things at this stage. But I do so want everything to be perfect.*" I wrote: *It's silly of me to question things* because I was applying the art of misdirection. In reality, had this been a more straightforward plot, I would probably have written: *It's silly of me to question myself...* or *it's silly of me to doubt myself at this stage.*

"*I left school at sixteen. Staying on to do A Levels wasn't an option for me. It's something I've come to regret over the years. No-one from my family has ever been to university. Until now.*" At this point in the story we are still maintaining the misdirection, whilst at the same time providing clues and an explanation of the protagonist's motivation. It is only in the last few paragraphs that the true situation is revealed to the reader.

Let's recap

How you misdirect your audience will vary depending on what kind of twist you have chosen. You need to write in such a way as to allow the story to make sense once the plot twist is revealed. Your readers will be able to glance back at the various points in the story that have created the misdirection and see that you have written honestly (if not openly). It's best to let the readers make their own assumptions about your characters and what is happening in the story—but whatever you do, don't resort to trickery or telling lies.

Remember the pictorial illusion we looked at earlier? When you present your readers with a story, you may want them to view a character as a 'young woman' and only point out the 'old woman' at the end. However, the clues should always be there—both in pictorial illusions and twist stories. It's simply a matter of knowing where to look.

PLOTS AND CHARACTER STEREOTYPES TO AVOID

It's said that all of the stories ever written can be boiled down into seven basic plots. Bringing something new to fiction is about applying your own unique style and voice to a story and—when it comes to plot twists—pushing yourself to think beyond your first few ideas.

Many magazines welcome short twist story submissions from writers, but there are some plots that seem to be written over and over and over again. Editors who pick up a story submission only to discover that it's another one of those oh-so-predictable plots must want to scream. At the very least, they probably roll their eyes before throwing the story onto the rejection pile and moving on to the next one.

Here are a few plot twists that have been used so often they have become clichés. This is not an exhaustive list but if the story you were planning to write fits into any of these categories, I'd recommend that you think again.

Six twists to avoid

1. Stories in which the main character turns out to be a dog, cat, parrot, or any other animal or inanimate object.

2. The main character suspects her husband is having an affair, only to discover that the beautiful blonde he is meeting is a party planner who is helping him to organise a surprise party for the main character's birthday.

3. Murder victims who are fed poisonous mushrooms, weed killer or equally unlikely methods of murder. Try to find a more original weapon or cause of death.

4. Old ladies who, rather than being the victim, turn out to be the criminal. Technically, this may be a reversal of identity, but innocent looking old lady characters have definitely been over-used.

5. Plots that rely on twins to explain the twist. To be frank, it's a bit of a con and a lazy way to deliver a twist. That's not to say that featuring identical twins is a total no-no—just be aware that you will have to be up-front about the twins' existence and apply an original treatment to this twist. When I read *Gone Girl* I was suspicious of Nick Dunne's twin sister, Margo. Early on in the novel I wondered whether Margo really existed, or whether Nick Dunne was suffering from dual personality disorder and Margo was his 'other self'. As it turned out, I had no reason to be suspicious. Margo was a character in her own right—but I was suspicious because of the widely acknowledged over-use of twins as a plot device.

6. Stories about murdering elderly relatives in order to get an inheritance, only to be thwarted in some way.

To dream or not to dream?

The worst, most clichéd twist of all is the one where the dramatic sequence of events that unfold in the early part of a story turn out to be a dream. Your main character, Arnold, is facing an impossible dilemma or task... your reader is on the edge of his seat wondering how Arnold will overcome the problem... and then Arnold wakes up and realises it has all been a dream. This is the worst kind of story—the sort an eight-year-old would tell, or someone who has 'written themselves into a corner' and hasn't the imagination to find out way of it. I would say, categorically, that there is no chance of getting that type of story published. Then again, if you're old enough, you may remember the shower scene in the TV show *Dallas* which heralded the return of Bobby. A whole season of programmes was explained as 'being a dream'!

By the way, it's OK to include dream sequences within a story—many writers have used this technique in novels and films, particularly in the thriller, horror, crime and mystery genres. The secret with dream sequences is to make sure they add something to the story. You should also make it clear to the reader when something *is* a dream. A dream sequence can be used to show a flashback, or to foreshadow future events. The difference is that these scenes form part of the whole story and aren't used as an easy way to get the character out of a hole.

Used carefully and sparingly, dream sequences within the storyline can enhance a piece of fiction. However, the technique of using dreams to show a flashback or a premonition has become a little dated and, for that reason, seems to be employed less often these days, especially in films.

NOVEL V SHORT STORY

There is no doubt that twists can work really well in short stories. The format is the perfect length to deliver a clever twist quickly, and just long enough to be able to integrate clues, create signposts and sustain a misdirection. The vast majority of twists in short stories come at the end.

However, for all of you budding novelists out there, I'm pleased to report that twist plots are equally popular with novel readers as they are with readers of short fiction. Novels with a twist have been around for a long time. Think about the shocking revelation part way through Charlotte Bronte's *Jane Eyre*, when it is revealed that the first Mrs Rochester is alive (if not well) and living in the attic at Thornfield Hall. That twist explains the mysterious happenings that have taken place earlier in the story, but it also takes the novel and the relationship between Jane Eyre and Edward Rochester in a whole new direction.

Plot twists feature regularly in contemporary works of fiction. Recently, I finished a novel called *Tideline* by Penny Hancock. It's a beautifully written psychological thriller that includes an unexpected twist towards the end that I certainly didn't see coming. Then there are the novels that deliver a string of twists and turns and take the reader on an exhilarating journey of tension, conflict and intrigue.

That's the thing about plot twists in novels: they don't necessarily have to come at the end. If you want to, you can keep twisting the story around—first one way and then the other. I'd caution against delivering a twist too early. My view is that you should first give your readers a chance to engage with the story's characters. Plot twists have more impact once readers have begun to connect with the characters and think that they know them. Once they start to care about what happens to the protagonist, your audience will be affected by any surprises you inject as you twist and turn your plot. A twist can be introduced subtly to reveal character, or it can be a major, hit-the-reader-between-the-eyes shift that changes the course of the whole story.

One other piece of advice: avoid having *too many* twists in your novel. This can grow tiresome and confusing. Your readers may even start to anticipate the next twist as they read through the book and, inevitably, that is going to reduce the effectiveness of the 'surprise factor' in your plot.

There are clever twists, and twists that are pure genius. There are also writers who introduce twists in order to make themselves look clever. Always aim for the former and do everything you can to avoid the latter.

Whether you are writing flash fiction, a short story, or a novel, the twists you weave into the storyline must form an integral part of the plot and not be included merely to impress or thrown in as an added 'bonus'.

For most writers, the idea for the twist comes first and the story is built around it. This means that the twist lies (often hidden) at the heart of the story. Occasionally, short story writers or novelists will think of a twist as they are part way through writing a story. When that happens, they may have to go back and rework or adjust their plot, characterisation and dialogue to accommodate the twist and not make it obvious until it's time for the 'big reveal'.

As you become more involved in writing twist plots, you will become more adept at guessing the endings in the stories and novels you read, and in the films that you watch too. Will this spoil your enjoyment? Well... maybe a little. When you start to *think* like a writer, it becomes harder to find a plot surprise that will keep you guessing until the end. When you do encounter a film or story that delivers a twist you didn't guess, you will be all the more impressed!

Writing exercise

Now that you've learned how to sow clues and misdirect readers, you are in a better position to tackle your first twist story. Using the idea you created earlier, I want you to develop the first draft of a short story or the first three chapters of a novel. You may wish to use the framework headings from the 'Creating an Outline' chapter as a template. However, some writers find that planning stifles their creativity. If you are the kind of writer who prefers to launch straight into your story without any kind of outline, go ahead. Whichever approach you take, try to keep on writing straight through to the end of the story or the three chapters, rather than going back to review and edit your work.

Once you've finished writing this first draft, put your work aside for a few days, or longer if you can spare the time. When you revisit the manuscript you will be in a better position to review and edit your work more objectively.

EDITING AND PROOFREADING YOUR WORK

Before you submit your work to an editor, publisher or agent, or before deciding to self-publish your work in print or eBook format, you should make sure it is the very *best* it can be—and that means taking time out to edit and proofread your work thoroughly.

When to edit

Writing your first draft should be about focusing your energies wholly on the process of *creation*. During this initial (and sometimes tentative) stage of the writing, concentrate purely on telling the story. Let it out. Don't suppress or censor your imagination—simply go with the flow. Don't be tempted to stop to correct yourself or go back and edit the story before you've reached the end. If you do, you run the risk of never getting the first draft finished. In my experience, writing a first draft is much easier if you prepare a brief story outline first. However, I accept that not everyone is like me. You may be one of the many writers who abhor the idea of working to a plan.

The serious business of editing comes *after* you have completed the first draft. Editing is about taking a rough gem of a story and, through a process of cutting, shaping and refining, turning it into a polished product that you can be proud of.

Editing your work

All first drafts (and many second and third drafts) will need editing. It is a vitally important stage, and one that will usually take much longer than writing the first draft. If you want your story to shine, you have to be willing to polish your work and check it for errors.

As long as you're not working to a tight deadline, the best approach to editing is to give yourself plenty of time for reflection. Put the work aside and revisit it a few days or weeks later. This will allow you to view your story through fresh eyes and be more objective about what you have written. You'll be better placed to spot the weak parts and identify (and keep) the good bits.

Begin by thinking about the overall 'big picture'. Ask the following questions of your story:

- Does the opening work well? Is it likely to engage the reader and make them want to read on?
- Is your story well-structured? Have you told it in the right order? Does it hold together? Does it flow? Is it logical?
- Are your characters worth reading about? Will they provoke an emotional response (either positive or negative) in the readers?
- Have you managed to misdirect your readers successfully?
- Have you given them some clues?
- Are you happy with the twist and the ending?
- If you only have one twist, would it be possible to add a second or even a third twist?

Once you're happy with the overall shape and structure of your story or novel, it's time to work on the detail. Go back to the beginning and work through it, word by word, line by line and (if it's a novel) chapter by chapter. Get rid of unnecessary words and overlong sentences and look out for the following:

1. **Word repetition**: have you repeated the same or similar words in a sentence or paragraph? Can you use another word, or could you rework the sentence to remove the need for repetition?

2. **Pet words**: Like many writers, I'm guilty of using certain words a lot. As I edit a manuscript I look out for my 'pet' words which include 'just', 'really', 'actually' and 'particularly'. When I find them, I remove as many of them as possible. If *you* have a habit of over-using certain words, search for them and delete as many as you can bear to part with.

3. **Other repetitions**: have you wasted words by repeating the same information, facts or dialogue in different parts of your story? Are there any sections where you tell readers something for a second time, albeit in a different way? You may have chosen to do this on purpose (for emphasis) but if not, get rid of the repetition.

4. **Dialogue**: the dialogue in your story should do one (or more) of three things: reveal information, develop characterisation, or move the plot forward. If you hit a long section of dialogue in your manuscript that doesn't serve any of those functions, you should seriously consider removing it.

5. **Clichés**: it's easy to let tired or well-worn phrases slip into your sentences: leaving them there is a sign of sloppy writing. Get rid of clichés during the edit.

6. **Tautologies**: tautologies are words that repeat the same thing. For example: *She gave a loud scream*. Loudness is implicit in the word 'scream': there is no need to say 'loud' in this sentence ('a loud scream' is a tautology). Better to simply say: *She screamed.*

7. **Adverbs**: adverbs are words or phrases that are used to describe or modify the meaning of a verb, adjective, or another adverb. For example, you could say: *The horse ran quickly across the field*. The adverb here is *quickly*. If you need to save on words or you want to be more precise, you could say the following instead: *The horse galloped across the field*. That works so much better, doesn't it?

8. **Inconsistencies**: make sure that the later parts of your story don't contradict the earlier parts. These kind of mistakes are known as 'continuity errors' and refer to inconsistencies in characteristics, setting and appearance. If your main character is wearing a blue dress at the beginning of the chapter, don't describe her wearing a pair of jeans and a t-shirt later on (unless you have explained the reason for the wardrobe change). If you tell us a character is unfit, don't have them running up a hill later on in the story (unless you also show them pausing for breath half way up, or holding their side because they have a stitch).

9. **Story order**: Are you telling the story in a way that delivers the greatest impact? This is especially important if you are writing a longer piece of fiction that includes a number of sub-plots or is told from several viewpoints. If you finish one chapter on a cliffhanger, you can maximise the suspense by keeping your readers waiting. Rather than reveal what happens next, you

could instead weave in a chapter told from another character's viewpoint to move the focus to the sub-plot and away from the main action.

10. **Word choices**: Do the words you have chosen say *exactly* what you want to say? There are over one million words in the English language—careful selection will help you to establish your writing voice. Finding the right word to describe a scene or character can be a challenge, but one that is not unpleasant. Aim to use words that are clear, distinctive, memorable, or entertaining to bring each scene in your story to life.

Twist checks

As you proofread a piece of twist fiction, always be alert for clues that don't make sense or give away too much. Unlike the readers of your story, *you* will know exactly *when* you are introducing important information or foreshadowing events. As the story's creator you are in a position to understand exactly what is going on, but will the readers? Are they likely to recognise the clues and understand their significance, even if only with hindsight. Do your misdirections work? Are they too subtle or are they clumsy and obvious? Is the twist or surprise ending believable, or is it too contrived or clichéd?

Proofreading your work

When writers become entrenched in the creative process, they sometimes become blind to the words on the page. Because we are so familiar with the manuscript, it's easy to overlook typos and other errors. As we check through our work, there is a tendency to read what we *think* we have written, rather than what's actually on the page. Here are a few tips and ideas that will make the proofreading process a little easier.

The spell checker is your friend: Begin by checking your manuscript using your word processor's spell checker. Although you can't rely on it to point out *all* of your mistakes, it will highlight the obvious faults in your manuscript, so it's a sensible place to start.

Print out your story: After you've run a spell check, print out a copy of your story. Proofreading from a hard copy is much, much easier than checking your work on screen. You're far more likely to spot mistakes on a paper version of your manuscript and you can use the printed copy to mark up any changes or make notes.

Retreat to a quiet place: When proofreading, it's important to focus on the job in hand. A momentary lapse in concentration can lead to an error slipping through. For this reason, it's best to remove yourself from distractions and read your work somewhere quiet—away from the noise of TV, background music, or talkative friends or family.

Say it out loud: Reading your work aloud will help you find and fix misplaced commas, missing questions marks, and overlong or awkwardly constructed sentences. If a sentence is so long that you struggle to breathe as you read it, you can guarantee your readers will have the same problem. Another advantage to reading your work out loud is that it will help you to check whether your dialogue sounds natural.

Get someone else to check your work: It's amazing how quickly a fresh pair of eyes will spot errors that you have overlooked. Recruit someone who has a good grasp of spelling and grammar and an eye for detail and ask them (or pay them) to proofread your work.

Homonyms and homophones: Pay special attention to words that share the same spelling or pronunciation but have different meanings. For example: *wear* and *where*, *there* and *their*, *new* and *knew*, *compliment* and *complement*. These words won't get picked up by the spell checker, so look out for them as you read through your manuscript. Because they *sound* exactly the way they should, they can be difficult to spot (even if you read them aloud).

Clichés: You should aim to eradicate clichés during the editing process, but the final proofread provides one last chance to spot any that you may have missed.

Consistency: Complete the final checks for consistency and continuity. This could be in the spelling of a name—for instance, if you introduce a character called Fay in the first chapter, make sure she isn't called Faye in chapter six. This may sound obvious, but it's very easy for small errors to creep into your manuscript, especially when your work has been through several edits.

Proofreading may seem like a tiresome chore, but it *is* important. Once you've finished your story or novel, you will be eager to submit your manuscript in a bid to get it published. However, before you send your work to an editor, publisher or agent, you should take the time to check it thoroughly. By eliminating spelling mistakes and grammatical errors, you will add an extra layer of professionalism to your work and make a good first impression.

Proofreading exercise

This short exercise is designed to test your proofreading skills. Read through the extract below and see if you can spot a total of 24 spelling and grammatical errors. Once you have completed the exercise, read on to check your answers and read the story in full.

A Head of My Time by Jane Bettany

It was the greatest event of my live and I couldn't believe it was hear. I felt myself immerge from the blackness of oblivion, from the dark depths of nothingness—freed from the cold clutch of death. Struggling slowly back to life, I strived to recollect who I was and what had happened to me. And then, my eyes opened and I remembered.

My name was Melinda Fretson. I was born in 1951 and died in the year 2000. That much, at least, I could recall. But how long had I waited for this rebirth? Ten years? A hundred. A thousand maybe? How long had I been frozen in time?

Bright, blinding sunlight steamed through the windows of the room in which I lay, bouncing off the plane white walls and warming me a little. A woman sat in the corner and, on seeing me stirr, she gave a dazzling smile and rushed to my side.

"Welcome back, Malinda," she said, touching my forhead and glancing breifly at a row of beeping, digital moniters above my head. Seemingly satisfied, she smiled again and said: "I'll fetch the doctor."

With that, she left me alone in the silent, empty room, and carefully—as if they were delicate, dusty antiques—I began to re-examine my store of memories to recall how this whole thing had happened.

I'd first read about cryonics back in the early 1990s. One of the sunday newspapers had interviewed a family whose bodies were to be frozen after there death in the hope that, eventually, technology would be able to bring them back to life. Initially, I'd scoughed at the idea, thinking it ludicrous. How could people be brought back from the dead. It simply wasn't possible.

It was my daughter, Lisa, who changed my mind. When I showed her the article she was really interested.

"They put a man on the moon didn't they?" she said. "Who would have believed that a hundred years ago? Anything is possible, given time."

She found out as much as she could about cryonics until, one day, she told me she'd found a american company that could arrange everything. There consultant came to see us, armed with glossie brochures and eager to answer our questions. He explained that, after we died, our body's would be injected with preservatives and flewn to an abandoned salt mine in Arizona. And their we would remain, frozen, until sceince had advanced suffisiently to bring us back.

Now read the full story

How did you do? Was the proofreading exercise easy or hard? Were the errors difficult to find?

Spelling mistakes are often easier to spot than grammatical errors. Missing question marks, for instance, are frequently overlooked—which is why reading your work aloud can be so useful.

If you are intrigued by the opening section of this short twist story and would like to read the rest of it, turn to the next page where you will find the full (proof checked) version.

A Head of My Time by Jane Bettany

It was the greatest event of my life and I couldn't believe it was here. I felt myself emerge from the blackness of oblivion, from the dark depths of nothingness—freed from the cold clutch of death. Struggling slowly back to life, I strived to recollect who I was and what had happened to me. And then, my eyes opened and I remembered.

My name was Melinda Fretson. I was born in 1951 and died in the year 2000. That much, at least, I could recall. But how long had I waited for this rebirth? Ten years? A hundred? A thousand maybe? How long had I been frozen in time?

Bright, blinding sunlight streamed through the windows of the room in which I lay, bouncing off the plain white walls and warming me a little. A woman sat in the corner and, on seeing me stir, she gave a dazzling smile and rushed to my side.

"Welcome back, Melinda," she said, touching my forehead and glancing briefly at a row of beeping, digital monitors above my head. Seemingly satisfied, she smiled again and said: "I'll fetch the doctor."

With that, she left me alone in the silent, empty room, and carefully—as if they were delicate, dusty antiques—I began to re-examine my store of memories to recall how this whole thing had happened.

I'd first read about cryonics back in the early 1990s. One of the Sunday newspapers had interviewed a family whose bodies were to be frozen after their death in the hope that, eventually, technology would be able to bring them back to life.

Initially, I'd scoffed at the idea, thinking it ludicrous. How could people be brought back from the dead? It simply wasn't possible. It was my daughter, Lisa, who changed my mind. When I showed her the article she was really interested.

"They put a man on the moon didn't they?" she said. "Who would have believed that a hundred years ago? Anything is possible, given time."

She found out as much as she could about cryonics until, one day, she told me she'd found an American company that could arrange everything. Their consultant came to see us, armed with glossy brochures and eager to answer our questions. He explained that, after we died, our bodies would be injected with preservatives and flown to an abandoned salt mine in Arizona. And there we would remain, frozen, until science had advanced sufficiently to bring us back.

It seemed bizarre. Surreal almost.

We tried to discuss it with our family and friends but, without exception, they disapproved. By then, Lisa and I didn't care. We were determined to go ahead.

"We can freeze your whole body or just your head," the consultant told us.

For me, that was the easiest decision of all. I'd never been happy with the plump physique that fate had landed me with, so I opted to have only my head frozen.

"In the next life, I'd like a slimmer, more shapely body."

"It's not going to be the next life, Mum," Lisa said. "Just a continuation of this one. The most important thing is that we'll have one another. We'll be in it together."

We were given special bracelets to wear, to identify us when the time came. And we were each given a number. Mine was H1072, and it was tattooed behind my right ear. Lisa had decided to have her whole body frozen. Her number B2001, was tattooed on the inside of her wrist.

We had to take out an insurance policy to pay for the cost of freezing. It wasn't cheap; but you know what they say—you can't take it with you. And now, here I was, with a slim, healthy body and a whole new life ahead of me.

A door opened to my left and the nurse reappeared, followed by another woman—presumably the doctor.

"I'm Dr Daniels," she told me. "How are you feeling?"

"A little strange," I said. "How long have I been frozen? What year is this?"

"The year is 2148," the doctor replied. "Cryonic rebirth is still in its infancy. It's only recently that we've managed to perfect the process. You've been frozen for a long time. We weren't sure how well you'd come through it... or if you'd be able to remember anything."

"I can remember... almost everything."

"Can you remember how you died?"

I tried to retrieve the memory, but it drifted in the shadows of my consciousness, just out of reach.

"I can recall everything up until that point. I remember that my daughter and I had gone out for the day. Where is my daughter? Is she here?"

An expression of sympathy and distaste flickered in the nurse's eyes. The doctor took my hand.

"It's probably a good thing that you can't remember how you died," she said. "You see, it was an accident. The records tell us that you and your daughter were in your car. There was a collision..."

"Did my daughter die as well?"

"Yes, I'm afraid she did."

A pain gripped my chest; the sharp, searing ache of sorrow and loss. Tears welled in my eyes and ran down my cheeks. A cry of agony began to form in my throat. And then I remembered.

My daughter had died, and so had I. But we had both opted for cryonics. There was no need to mourn. The thought quelled my grief and, for one brief moment, I felt elated—until I looked at the doctor's face.

She squeezed my hand. "Your daughter sustained some very bad head injuries. I'm afraid that we weren't able to bring her back.... at least not completely. But I want you to know that we tried. We did everything we could."

"She's dead? She isn't here to share this with me?" Fear raced through my new veins. "I'm here all alone?"

Tears dripped onto my cheeks and I lifted my hand to wipe them away. It was then that a scream of pure horror erupted from my mouth and the greatest event of my life became the worst moment of a living death.

Because there, tattooed on the inside of my pale, slender wrist was a number. B2001

SUBMITTING YOUR WORK

Once you have completed your short story or novel and have edited and proof checked it carefully, you will be ready to send it off. How you submit your work will depend on whether you are writing a short story or a novel. Let's begin with how to submit short stories.

Short fiction

With a short story, you will most likely be submitting it to the editor of a magazine. Before you send your work, ask yourself the following questions:

- Does the story match the editor's guidelines for the magazine you're sending it to?
- Is it the right word count?
- Is it written in a style that suits the target audience of the magazine?

If you answer 'no' to any of these questions, then you will need to revise your story (or your choice of magazine) before going ahead and sending it off.

Many magazines still prefer to receive story manuscripts by post in hard copy format. Some do accept email submissions, but you should check the magazine's guidelines to find out whether this is the case. You should be able to find submission guidelines on the magazine's website and these will usually include details of how the manuscript should be laid out. Follow the submission instructions carefully.

The general rule for formatting is to print the manuscript in double-spacing using generous margins on all four sides. Print on one side of the paper only and don't forget to include page numbers.

Once you've sent off your manuscript, you should turn your attentions to writing your next twist story. Don't waste time worrying about the fate of the story you've submitted. Magazine editors are notoriously busy and it could be many weeks (sometimes several months) before you hear back from them. Generally speaking, most magazines will give you a decision on your story within 8 to 10 weeks. If they are very busy or have received an unusually high number of unsolicited manuscripts, it could be as long as five to six months before you hear anything.

If you don't want to wait that long, it's OK to chase up an editor if they've had your story for 12 weeks or more. Send a polite but brief email or letter that says something like this:

I submitted a short story called [insert the title of your story here] to you on [insert date] and thought I would check that it has arrived safely. If you have not received the manuscript, please let me know and I will resend it. Thank you for your time. I'll wait to hear your decision once you've had a chance to read the story.

Some writers worry that chasing a submission in this way may harm their chances of acceptance. In my experience, it doesn't. If you've written a great twist story that is perfect for the magazine, the editor will want to buy it, regardless of whether you've sent a reminder.

Novels

If you have written a novel, you will have to decide whether you are going to try and find an agent, or submit it directly to a publisher. However, it's important to remember that some publishing houses will not accept unsolicited manuscripts or proposals—they only consider work submitted through an agent.

Agents work on your behalf to sell your book and get the best deal they can for you (and of course they take a fee). The trouble is, it can be as hard to get an agent as it is to sell your work directly to a publisher—and even if you are able to get an agent, there is no guarantee that they will be able to sell your work. So, what is the best approach? My recommendation is that you:

- Start by checking which publishing houses or imprints publish the kind of book that you have written. If it's a romantic comedy with a twist, or a crime novel, or an historical mystery, go to your local library and take a look at books in those genres. Turn to the reverse of the book's title page and you should find the publisher's details and often their website address. Make a note of this information.

- Next, go to the publishers' websites to see whether they accept submissions from authors, or whether you will need to submit via an agent. If they will consider unsolicited manuscripts, check the submission guidelines online. These will explain the process for submitting your work.

- If you are looking for a literary agent, I suggest you check the *Writers' & Artists' Yearbook* published by Bloomsbury (if you're in the UK) or *Writer's Market* published by

Writer's Digest Books (if you're in the US or Canada). These useful publications include lists of magazine and book publishers and literary agents, as well as tips on getting published. The agent listings include details of the style of writing or genre each agent is willing to represent (such as crime fiction, literary fiction, fantasy, science fiction etc). Website details are also listed, which will provide you with further advice and information.

- Whether you are submitting directly to a publisher or through an agent, initially you will most likely need to submit only a synopsis of your novel and the first three chapters—but check for individual requirements, as some publishers and agents prefer to see completed manuscripts. Usually though, they will only ask to see the rest of the book if they like the look of the first three chapters and your synopsis. I'm not going to provide advice on how to write a synopsis for your novel because there are already plenty of books and websites that cover this subject in depth, including some that also offer advice on writing query letters to agents and publishers.

As with submitting short stories, once you have sent off your submission to an agent or publisher, you will have to play the waiting game. Use this time to focus your energies on starting a new writing project.

Tips for formatting your manuscript

The process of formatting your manuscript is pretty much the same for both novels and short stories. First and foremost, you should lay out your work based on the recommendations in the guidelines provided by the editor, publisher or agent you are submitting to. If there are no guidelines, or they are not specific, you can use the following general guide to prepare your manuscript.

Clear and easy to read: It's important to make your finished manuscript clear and easy to read. You should use a standard font such as Times New Roman, Arial or Tahoma in font size 12 or 13, and avoid script fonts, as these can be difficult to read.

Print your story on one side of the paper only: No double-sided printing (even if it does save paper). Set your text in double-spacing, indenting each new paragraph, and include generous margins. Use a standard paper size such as A4 or letter size.

Insert a cover sheet at the front of the manuscript: This should show your name (and pen name if you intend to use one). You should also include your address, email address, the title of your story or novel, plus the word count (or expected total word count if you are submitting only the first three chapters of a novel).

The first page of each short story or chapter should begin half way down the page: Start the first line just above the middle of the page, printing in double-line spacing. Page numbers are vital, and it's also a good idea to include a header or footer with your name and the title of the story or novel. At the very end of your short story or novel type the word END, centred on the page.

Keep a record: Make sure you keep a record of where you send your work and keep track of when it is returned.

At the end of this chapter you will find an example of the layout for a short story (I have included an example cover sheet, the first page of the story, the second page, and an example last page). You can use a similar layout if you are submitting a novel, making sure that you start each new chapter on a new page.

Dealing with self-doubt

Submitting your work for the first time can be nerve-wracking. Some writers feel overly protective of their stories and may be reluctant to send them off into the finicky world of publishing. Letting go of your 'baby' can be difficult because it can give rise to a sense of self-doubt and apprehension. What if the editor hates your writing? How will you cope if the novel you have worked on for two years is rejected?

These are perfectly natural questions but there are no simple answers. Being a writer is a tough gig and succeeding isn't easy. All you can ask of yourself is that you do your very best to produce the finest piece of fiction that you can.

Don't give up, even if your work is rejected. Pick yourself up, sulk for a while if you have to (but not for too long) and then keep on writing.

A Head of My Time

by

Jane Bettany

Short story: 1,060 words

Jane Bettany
My address
Town or City
County or State
Post code or Zip code

Tel: 01234 567890
Email: name@mailingaddress.com

MANUSCRIPT EXAMPLE (FIRST PAGE)

Jane Bettany
My address
Town or City
County or State
Post code or Zip code

A Head of My Time

by

Jane Bettany

It was the greatest event of my life and I couldn't believe it was here. I felt myself emerge from the blackness of oblivion, from the dark depths of nothingness – freed from the cold clutch of death. Struggling slowly back to life, I strived to recollect who I was and what had happened to me. And then, my eyes opened and I remembered.

My name was Melinda Fretson. I was born in 1951 and died in the year 2000. That much, at least, I could recall. But how long had I waited for this rebirth? Ten years? A hundred? A thousand maybe? How long had I been frozen in time?

Bright, blinding sunlight streamed through the windows of the room in which I lay, bouncing off the plain white walls and warming me a little. A woman sat in the corner and, on seeing me stir, she gave a dazzling smile and rushed to my side.

"Welcome back, Melinda," she said, touching my forehead and glancing briefly at a row of beeping, digital monitors above my head. Seemingly satisfied, she smiled again and said: "I'll fetch the doctor."

With that, she left me alone in the silent, empty room, and carefully – as if they were delicate, dusty antiques – I began to re-examine my store of memories to recall how this whole thing had happened.

I'd first read about cryonics back in the early 1990s. One of the Sunday newspapers had interviewed a family whose bodies were to be frozen after their death in the hope that, eventually, technology would be able to bring them back to life.

Initially, I'd scoffed at the idea, thinking it ludicrous. How could people be brought back from the dead? It simply wasn't possible. It was my daughter, Lisa, who changed my mind. When I showed her the article she was really interested.

"They put a man on the moon didn't they?" she said. "Who would have believed that a hundred years ago? Anything is possible, given time."

She found out as much as she could about cryonics until, one day, she told me she'd found an American company that could arrange everything. Their consultant came to see us, armed with glossy brochures and eager to answer our questions. He explained that, after we died, our bodies would be injected with preservatives and flown to an abandoned salt mine in Arizona. And there we would remain, frozen, until science had advanced sufficiently to bring us back.

It seemed bizarre. Surreal almost.

MANUSCRIPT EXAMPLE (LAST PAGE)

"She's dead? She isn't here to share this with me?" Fear raced through my new veins. "I'm here all alone?"

Tears dripped onto my cheeks and I lifted my hand to wipe them away. It was then that a scream of pure horror erupted from my mouth and the greatest event of my life became the worst moment of a living death.

Because there, tattooed on the inside of my pale, slender wrist was a number. B2001.

END

SEVEN STEPS TO SUCCESS

I hope you are now feeling more confident about writing stories with a twist. When you read a book on writing or go along to an author event or conference it's easy to feel inspired and motivated to try something new or simply get on and finish an existing writing project. In order to keep that motivation going, you have to *take action*—so, now that you've reached the end of this book, here are a few suggested action points.

Step 1: Write up the story idea you came up with in the writing exercise. Don't worry if, ultimately, the story doesn't work out. Use it as a starting point to get you writing.

Step 2: Make use of the story framework headings if you think they will help you to plan and outline your story. I recommend creating an outline before starting to write—either a detailed plan, or a basic outline. However, if you prefer to write without a plan, go for it! Some people are stifled by having to create any kind of outline and prefer to write, from fresh, straight into their story.

Step 3: Bear in mind the six twist types, but don't let them restrict you. You are free to combine any number of twist types in your work. Doing this can often lead to some quirky and original stories.

Step 4: Remember to think about where you plan to sell your work once it is completed. This can help to keep your writing on track and give you a head start when it comes to getting it published.

Step 5: Put your first draft aside and revisit it with fresh perspective a few days or weeks later. Be ruthless when you edit your work. It's at this stage that you can turn mediocre fiction into something really special.

Step 6: Don't hold back when it comes to submitting your work. Overcome any fears you may have of rejection. Unless you are willing to put your work out there, you are never going to be published.

Step 7: Keep on writing and your confidence as a writer will grow. Putting time aside to write regularly will, eventually, pay dividends.

Recommended reading

Read as many twist stories as you can. Remember that you can learn as much from the ones that aren't so good as you can from the really brilliant ones. Here are a few titles to start you off:

Short Stories:

Completely Unexpected Tales: Tales of the Unexpected and More Tales of the Unexpected by Roald Dahl (ISBN 0140098208)

Stories by O Henry (ISBN 0812505026)

A Twist in the Tale by Jeffrey Archer (ISBN 1447221877)

A Twist of the Knife by Peter James (ISBN 144721210X)

The Withered Arm by Thomas Hardy (you should be able to download this from the internet as it is in the public domain)

Novels:

Gone Girl by Gillian Flynn (ISBN 1780228228)

Tideline by Penny Hancock (ISBN 0857206281)

Books on the craft of writing:

Becoming a Writer by Dorothea Brande (ISBN 9780874771640)

On Writing by Stephen King (ISBN 9781444723250)

The Writer's Digest Guide to Query Letters by Wendy Burt-Thomas (ISBN 9781582975665)

Guide to Literary Agents 2017 by Chuck Sambuchino (Ed) (ISBN 144034776X)

GLOSSARY OF TERMS

GLOSSARY

ANTAGONIST: An antagonist is a character who is hostile to, or opposes your main character (protagonist) as he tries to achieve his aims or objectives. Antagonists are often portrayed as nasty, difficult or even evil—but they don't have to be 'bad'. They could simply be a rival or create a problem that stands in the way of your main character reaching his goal.

CHEKHOV'S GUN: Chekhov's gun is a dramatic principle that requires that every part of a piece of fiction contributes in some way to the story. The term was coined by author Anton Chekhov who said: *"Remove everything that has no relevance to the story. If you say in the first chapter that there is a rifle hanging on the wall, in the second or third chapter it absolutely must go off. If it's not going to be fired, it shouldn't be hanging there."* The principle is described in more detail in the chapter on Sowing Clues.

COMEDY: The origins of the term 'comedy' are rooted in Ancient Greece, but its modern meaning refers to work intended to be humorous, create laughter or generally be amusing and entertaining.

DEUS EX MACHINA: This term translates as 'God from the machine'. It originated in Greek theatre where 'Gods' were often lowered onto the stage from a machine at the end of a play to resolve a problem. Today, the term refers to any contrived plot device that brings in an unexpected event, character or power to sort out a difficult or seemingly impossible situation.

DRAMATIC IRONY: Irony or dramatic irony occurs when the consequences of dialogue or a situation are understood by the readers or audience but not grasped by the fictional characters themselves.

FLASHBACK: In literature and film, flashbacks are the scenes that take the story narrative back from the current point in time to reflect on something that has happened in the past.

FORESHADOWING: Foreshadowing is another literary technique used by writers to drop hints or warnings about something that is going to happen further on in the story. It is most commonly used to arouse interest and entice people to read on.

IMPERATIVE: An imperative in fiction is something that is of vital importance to the story or plot. The presence of this 'imperative' is necessary to make the story work.

IRONY: See 'dramatic irony' above.

NON-LINEAR NARRATIVE: A non-linear narrative tells the story in a random, disrupted or disjointed order that does not follow the chronological sequence of events.

PERIPETEIA: A sudden or dramatic change of fortune that provides a turning point in fiction.

PROTAGONIST: This is another term that originated in Ancient Greece. Protagonist means "chief actor" or "player of the first part". Today, the term protagonist refers to the main character in a story, play or film and is likely to be the character that the audience identifies with most strongly.

PSYCHOLOGICAL THRILLER: Psychological thrillers are stories that focus on the psychology and emotional state of its characters. Psychological thrillers often include elements of crime, mystery or horror, with an emphasis on explaining or puzzling over *why* the characters do what they do.

PYRRHIC VICTORY: A Pyrrhic victory is a hollow or meaningless victory. Whilst technically, the victor may have won a battle or conflict, the terrible price they have had to pay for that victory takes away any sense of achievement.

REVERSAL OF ACHIEVEMENT: With this type of reversal the main character sets out to achieve something only to be thwarted by their circumstances or opposite character.

REVERSAL OF FORTUNE: A reversal of fortune (also known as peripeteia) brings a sudden change in fortune for the main character. Sometimes this is a positive change, sometimes it is a negative one.

REVERSAL OF IDENTITY: In stories that use a reversal of identity, one of the characters turns out to be someone or something else. This could be a hero that turns out to be a villain, or vice versa. As with a story told by an unreliable narrator, this kind of twist relies on readers making assumptions.

REVERSAL OF MOTIVE: A story that uses a reversal of motive leads the reader to believe that a character's actions are motivated by a certain goal, only to reveal that their actions are deceitful and their goal is completely different (and usually more malevolent). This kind of twist is commonly used in romantic suspense novels, or psychological thrillers.

REVERSAL OF PERCEPTION: A reversal of perception changes the way the main character (or the reader) perceives the story. This can be a perceptual shift in the way a character views the world. Sometimes the writer will play around with the reader's perception of a situation by introducing a non-linear narrative which uses a reverse chronology, or tell the story in a non-chronological order using flashbacks.

REVERSE CHRONOLOGY: With a reverse chronology the plot is revealed in reverse order. It is a story that is told backwards. The story begins with the final scene or event and then moves on by going back in time to show how the situation in the opening scene came about.

ROMANTIC SUSPENSE: Romantic suspense is a category of the romance genre that involves intrigue or a mystery that the main character must solve.

UNRELIABLE NARRATOR: An unreliable narrator tells a story that hides the truth.

ABOUT THE AUTHOR

Jane Bettany is a freelance writer, publisher and creative writing teacher with more than twenty years of writing experience. Her stories and non-fiction articles have appeared in women's magazines, literary magazines, newspapers and online.

Jane has an MA in Creative Writing and is a qualified teacher. She delivers creative writing classes in workshops, courses and online. You can follow Jane on Twitter @JaneBettany or on Facebook at www.facebook.com/WritingNetwork.

If you have enjoyed reading this book you may also be interested in *How to Write Short Stories That Sell* by Jane Bettany, which is available in paperback or as an eBook.

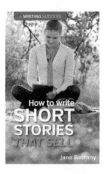

ISBN 9780957670433
Available from Amazon and all good bookshops

CPSIA information can be obtained
at www.ICGtesting.com
Printed in the USA
BVHW071743170419
545810BV00002B/215/P